25 MOST VALUABLE SHOR...

KEY	ACTION
↵	Chooses the currently highlighted menu command, or the default button in a dialog box.
Alt	Activates/deactivates the menu bar.
Alt+- (hyphen)	Opens the Control menu for a document window.
Alt+↵	Switches a DOS application between full-screen and window size (in 386 enhanced mode).
Alt+↓	Opens a Drop-Down list box.
Alt+F4	Closes the current application window—exits Windows if Program Manager is the current window.
Alt+ *letter*	Opens the menu with the underlined letter, or moves to dialog box option with underlined letter.
Alt+PrintScreen (or Alt+Shift+PrintScreen)	Copies the current application window to Clipboard.
Alt+Spacebar	Opens the Control menu for an application window.
Alt+Tab	Switches among open applications (Hold down Alt and press Tab repeatedly to cycle through).
Ctrl+←	Moves to the previous word in text.
Ctrl+→	Moves to the next word in text.
Ctrl+End	Moves to the end of a document.
Ctrl+Esc	Calls up Task List.
Ctrl+F4	Closes current document window.
Ctrl+Home	Moves to the top of a document.
Ctrl+Z (or Alt+Backspace)	Undoes most recent editing change.
End	Moves to the end of the line in text.
Esc (Escape)	Backs out of menu selections, or chooses Cancel from a dialog box.
F1	Help!
Home	Moves to the start of a line in a document.
PrintScreen (or Shift+PrintScreen)	Copies the entire screen to Clipboard.
Shift+Tab	Moves to the previous option in a dialog box.
Spacebar	In a dialog box, toggles a check box on and off.
Tab	Moves to the next option in a dialog box.

SYBEX *Running* **START** BOOKS

The SYBEX *Running Start* series offers busy, computer-literate people two books in one: a quick, hands-on tutorial guide to program essentials, and a comprehensive reference to commands and features.

The first half of each *Running Start* book teaches the basic operations and underlying concepts of the topic software. These lessons feature trademark SYBEX characteristics: step-by-step procedures; thoughtful, well-chosen examples; an engaging writing style; valuable Notes, Tips, and Warnings; and plenty of practical insights.

Once you've learned the basics, you're ready to start working on your own. That's where the second half of each *Running Start* book comes in. This alphabetical reference offers concise instructions for using program commands, dialog boxes, and menu options. With dictionary-style organization and headings, this half of the book is designed to give you fast access to information.

SYBEX is very interested in your reactions to the *Running Start* series. Your opinions and suggestions will help all of our readers, including yourself. Please send your comments to: SYBEX Editorial Department, 2021 Challenger Dr., Alameda, CA 94501.

WINDOWS 3.1 *Running* START

WINDOWS™ 3.1 *Running* START

ALAN SIMPSON

SYBEX®

San Francisco • Paris • Düsseldorf • Soest

Acquisitions Editor: Dianne King
Editor: James A. Compton
Technical Editor: Ellen Ferlazzo
Book Design and Chapter Art: Claudia Smelser
"Running Start" Icon Designer: Alissa Feinberg
Screen Graphics: John Corrigan, Cuong Le
Page Layout and Typesetting: Len Gilbert
Proofreader/Production Assistant: David Silva
Indexer: Matthew Spence
Cover Design and Illustration: Archer Design

Screen reproductions produced with Collage Plus.
Collage Plus is a trademark of Inner Media Inc.

SYBEX is a registered trademark of SYBEX Inc.

TRADEMARKS: SYBEX has attempted throughout this book to distinguish proprietary trademarks from descriptive terms by following the capitalization style used by the manufacturer.

SYBEX is not affiliated with any manufacturer.

Every effort has been made to supply complete and accurate information. However, SYBEX assumes no responsibility for its use, nor for any infringement of the intellectual property rights of third parties which would result from such use.

Library of Congress Card Number: 92-82839
ISBN: 0-7821-1159-9

Manufactured in the United States of America
10 9 8 7 6 5 4 3 2 1

To Susan, Ashley, and Alec

ACKNOWLEDGMENTS

My sincere thanks to all the people who helped create this book: Elizabeth Olson, who wrote most of the reference entries; Martha Mellor, who reviewed the hands-on lessons and provided many improvements; Dianne King, who originated the whole idea; Jim Compton, who helped develop the concept and also edited the manuscript; Ellen Ferlazzo, who made many valuable technical suggestions throughout the book; Dan Tauber, who did the same for the communications and multimedia sections; Claudia Smelser, who brought her considerable design skills to the project; Len Gilbert, who handled the desktop publishing; and David Silva, who brought a proofreader's eye to the final results. And thanks to all the gang at Waterside Productions. Finally, Microsoft Corporation's Public Relations Department provided timely software and support.

TABLE*of*CONTENTS

PART TWO   ALPHABETICAL REFERENCE

PREFACE

This book shows you how to use the most important features of Windows 3.1, and offers practical skills that you can apply to virtually all Windows 3.1 applications. It's designed to be used in two ways: first as a brief tutorial, to get you started working productively in the Windows environment; and then as a concise reference guide to all the most important Windows features, to be consulted as questions arise in your day-to-day work. You'll get the most out of this book if you're new to Windows but not an absolute beginner with personal computers.

Part I offers 10 easy lessons:

Lesson One: *Getting Around in Windows* covers basic skills for getting started, using a mouse, managing windows and icons, getting online help, and exiting Windows.

Lesson Two: *Running Applications* teaches you how to run Windows and DOS applications, how to switch from application to application, and how to keep under control a screen that's cluttered with applications.

Lesson Three: *Personalizing Your Desktop* teaches you how to tailor Windows 3.1 to your tastes, including choosing screen colors, a wallpaper, and a screen saver. You'll also learn how to assign custom sounds to Windows events.

Lesson Four: *Handy Applets for Getting Organized* shows you how to use the handy Cardfile, Calendar, and Calculator applications that came with your Windows 3.1 program.

Lesson Five: *Working with Text* uses the simple Write word processor, supplied with Windows, to teach you general techniques for working with text in all Windows applications, including the use of TrueType fonts and the special characters that are new to Windows 3.1.

Lesson Six: *Working with Pictures* shows you general techniques for working with pictures and graphics in Windows applications, and will show you some fancy things you can do with PaintBrush (even if you can't draw worth beans).

Lesson Seven: *Pulling It All Together with OLE* teaches you all about Object Linking and Embedding (OLE) and Object Packager, two of Windows 3.1's hottest new features for combining text, sound, and pictures in your documents.

Lesson Eight: *Using File Manager and Print Manager* teaches you the basics of using File Manager and Print Manager, and the new drag-and-drop shortcuts in Windows 3.1.

Lesson Nine: *Streamlining Windows* shows you how to save time and trouble by automating common tasks.

Lesson Ten: *Extra Goodies: Modems, Sound, and Multimedia* teaches you how to use optional equipment that you may have installed on your computer, such as a modem, sound card, and CD-ROM drive.

These lessons have been structured so that you can try out the examples on your own computer, but you don't need to do so in order to get the essential information they present. For anyone coming to Windows from the text-based DOS environment, the hands-on practice in working with the mouse offered here will be particularly valuable.

Part II is a concise alphabetical reference to Windows' major features and applications. In each entry you'll find step-by-step instructions, shortcuts, examples, and special tips. The goal of it all is to give you a *running start* with Windows 3.1.

PART I

STEP-BY-STEP
TUTORIAL

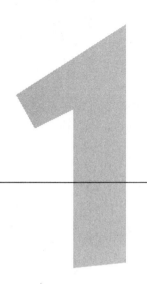

GETTING AROUND
IN WINDOWS

In this lesson, you'll learn the basics: how to start Windows, how to get around, how to open, close, size, and move windows, and how to get help when you need it. Let's begin with an overview of what's so special about Windows 3.1.

WHAT IS WINDOWS 3.1?

Windows 3.1 is a graphical operating environment for your PC. It offers several advantages over its predecessor, DOS.

Actually, Windows works in conjunction with DOS on your computer, and you can continue to use your DOS programs even when Windows is running.

Its most important features (some of which were introduced in Windows 3.0 and have been enhanced in this version) are these:

- **Graphical User Interface**: Windows offers a Graphical User Interface (GUI, pronounced "gooey") that is much more natural and intuitive than the text-based interface of DOS. The GUI is also a WYSIWYG (for what-you-see-is-what-you-get, pronounced *wizzy wig*) display that lets you see text and pictures on the screen, exactly as they will look when printed (see Figure 1.1).

- **Multitasking**: Whereas DOS generally lets you run only one application (program) at a time, you can run several applications at once in Windows—each in its own *window*.

- **Common User Access**: One of the problems in using DOS programs was that they all used different sets of menu commands, function keys, and the like. But all Windows applications follow a standard set of guidelines, called the Common User Access (CUA), which makes it easier to learn new applications and to switch from one application to another. Thanks to the CUA guidelines, the skills you develop working with the standard Windows applications over the following lessons will be easy to transfer to more sophisticated applications you'll run under Windows.

- **Easier Transfer of Data**: Unlike DOS, Windows makes it easy to transfer text, data, and pictures between applications.

FIGURE 1.1:

A sample document displayed in the DOS and Windows environments. The Windows environment lets you see the text and graphics as they will actually be printed.

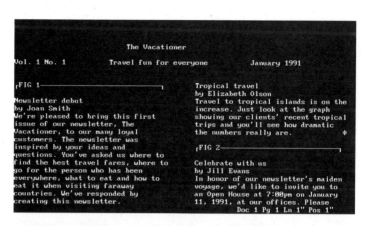

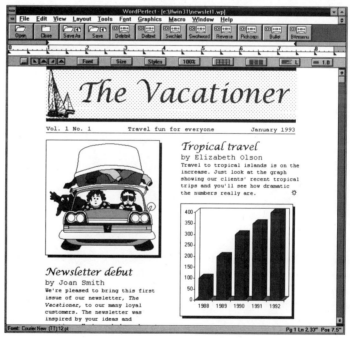

STARTING WINDOWS

Starting Windows is simple:

1. Start your computer in the usual manner, and get to the DOS command prompt (typically C:\>).

2. Type **win** and press ↵.

You should see a brief sign-on banner, followed by the Windows desktop and the Program Manager window, looking something like Figure 1.2. Your screen, however, might have a completely different background, and different icons within the Program Manager window. Nothing to worry about!

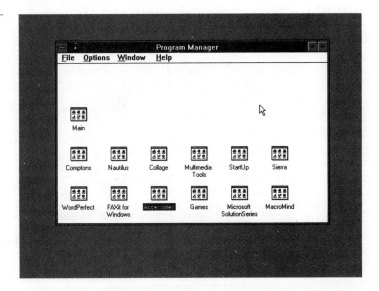

FIGURE 1.2:

Program Manager is the first application to appear when you successfully start Windows 3.1.

If the Program Manager initially appears as an icon near the lower left corner of the screen, double-click that icon.

USING THE MOUSE

You can use either the mouse or the keyboard to interact with Windows, but a mouse is much easier. If you've never used a mouse before, here's some standard mouse terminology to get you started:

- **Mouse button**: The "active" button on your mouse, where your index finger naturally rests. Normally, this is the left button, but it's the right button on a "left-handed" mouse.

- **Mouse pointer**: A small arrow on the screen that moves in whatever direction you move the mouse.

- **Click**: To *click* an item on the screen, roll the mouse until the pointer is on the item you want, then click the button.

- **Double-Click**: Move the pointer to the item you want, then click the button twice in rapid succession.

- **Drag (also called *Click-and-Drag*):** Move the pointer to the item you want, click the button and hold it down while you move the mouse, then release the button. The item will be dragged along with the pointer.

The mouse is much easier to get along with if you get a rubber mouse pad, rather than trying to roll it around on a slick desktop.

If you're new to using a mouse, it might feel a little awkward at first. You'll get some practice using the mouse later in this lesson and throughout the Step-by-Step portion of this book.

USING THE KEYBOARD

Using the keyboard in Windows is pretty much the same as in any other program. Combination keystrokes are indicated by a plus (+) sign between the keys, as in Ctrl+F4. To press a combination keystroke, you hold down the first key (Ctrl in this example), press the second key (F4 in this example), then release both keys.

WHAT IS A WINDOW?

Each application that you run in Windows runs within its own window—a framed portion of the screen. Thus, each window on your screen is your view into some application that's currently running. Most windows have the elements illustrated in Figure 1.3, which, as you'll learn in this lesson, make it easy to size and move windows, as well as access commands via menus.

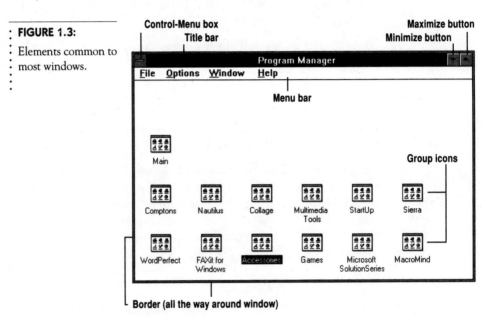

FIGURE 1.3:
Elements common to most windows.

There may already be one or more open windows inside your Program Manager window—Startup, if you've just installed Windows, or perhaps applications installed by other users of your computer. If your screen shows any open group windows right now, just click the open group window's Minimize button, or double-click its Control-Menu box, until only group icons appear, as in Figure 1.2.

If you click the Minimize button on the Program Manager window, that whole window will shrink to an icon. Double-clicking that icon will reopen the window.

USING THE MENU BAR

The menu bar near the top of a window displays the names of available menus. You can open any menu using either the mouse or the keyboard:

- To open a menu with your mouse, simply click its name.
- Or, to open a menu with the keyboard, hold down the Alt key, type the letter that's underlined in the menu name, then release both keys.
- Or, press and release the Alt key, then use the ← and → keys to highlight the name of the menu you want, then press ↵.

Once you've opened a menu, you can use the same techniques to choose a command from that menu. However, it's not necessary to hold down the Alt key when typing the underlined letter.

Commands that are dimmed on a menu are not appropriate for the current situation, and hence are not available for selection.

OUR CONVENTIONS FOR SHOWING A SEQUENCE OF MENU SELECTIONS

In this book we'll display a series of menu selections separated by the symbol ➤. For instance, this instruction:

- Choose **Window ➤ Arrange Icons**

means "Choose **Window** from the menu bar, then choose **Arrange Icons** from the menu that appears."

BACKING OUT OF MENU SELECTIONS

If you ever make a series of menu selections that lead you into unfamiliar territory, and want to back out gracefully without making any choices, just press Esc or click some neutral area outside the menu. If that doesn't work, try clicking the Cancel button if one is available.

TIDYING UP YOUR ICONS

If your icons are spread willy-nilly within the Program Manager, try the sample menu sequence above to have Windows arrange your icons more neatly:

◆ Choose **Window ➤ Arrange Icons**

Now your screen should look more like our initial Figure 1.2. But again, the exact icons displayed on your screen may be different.

SIZING AND MOVING WINDOWS

In addition to the menu bar, most windows contain a title bar, borders, and the buttons shown in Figure 1.3. These features let you move and size the window to your liking. To try them out:

1. Click the Maximize button in the upper right corner of the Program Manager. The window expands to full-screen size, and the Maximize button changes to a Restore button, with up- and down-pointing arrows.

2. Now click the Restore button in the upper right corner of the window. The window returns to its previous size.

You can also maximize or restore a window by double-clicking its title bar.

3. Click the window's Minimize button. The window shrinks to an icon in the lower left corner of the screen.

4. Double-click the Program Manager icon. The window reopens to its previous size.

Easy enough, no? Now let's try moving the window:

1. Move the mouse pointer into the title bar of the Program Manager window.

2. Hold down the mouse button, and drag the outline that appears to some new location on your screen.

3. Release the mouse button.

That was easy, too. Now repeat those steps to put the window wherever you really want it to be. Next we'll try sizing the window from one of its corners:

1. Move the mouse pointer to the lower right corner of the window, until the pointer turns into a two-headed arrow.

2. Hold down the mouse button, and drag the corner up to the opposite corner, until the frame is about half the size of the window.

3. Release the mouse button.

TIP

You can move the mouse pointer to any edge or corner of the window, until it becomes a two-headed arrow, then drag the mouse to size the window from there.

Now your window might look more like Figure 1.4, with *scroll bars* at the bottom and right edges. (If your window does not contain at least one scroll bar, shrink it some more).

FIGURE 1.4:

The Program Manager shrunk to the point that scroll bars appear at the bottom and right edges.

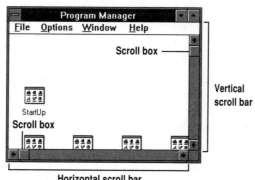

USING SCROLL BARS

Scroll bars are your indication that a window contains more information than it can display at once. In our Program Manager window, you can use the scroll bars to bring any hidden icons into view, using any of the following methods:

- Click the arrows at the ends of the scroll bar to scroll a small amount at a time.

- Or, drag the scroll box to a position in the scroll bar corresponding to the general location where you want to work.

- Or, click anywhere within the scroll bar to move one window at a time.

Assuming you've reduced the size of the window enough to show one or more scroll bars, you can experiment with them right now on your own. When you're done experimenting, put the Program Manager back in order:

1. Resize the Program Manager window again so that it's large enough to display all of its icons (just drag any corner to resize the window, and drag the window's title bar, if necessary, to move the window).

2. To rearrange icons in the resized window, choose **Window ➤ Arrange Icons** again.

OPENING GROUP WINDOWS

Each icon within the Program Manager is a *group icon*, so named because each contains a group of additional icons. You open a group in the same way you open any icon, by double-clicking it. Let's try it with the Accessories group:

1. Move the mouse pointer to the Accessories icon.

2. Double-click that icon.

If it didn't work, try again, making sure the mouse pointer is touching the Accessories icon, and that your double-click is quick.

Notice that, unlike the Program Manager, which contains *group icons* that all look alike, the Accessories group window contains *application icons*. Each icon represents an application that you can open.

Notice also that the Accessories group window does not contain a menu bar. That's because, unlike the Program Manager, which is an *application window*, Accessories is a *document window*. Though the basic mouse techniques for moving and sizing application windows and document windows are virtually the same, a few differences are worth noting:

♦ An application window contains a menu bar; a document window has no menu bar.

♦ An application window can be moved and sized anywhere on the screen, but a document window can only be moved and sized within its application window.

♦ When you minimize a document window, its icon falls within the larger application window, rather than at the lower left corner of the desktop.

♦ When you maximize a document window, its title bar disappears, and its name appears in the application window's title bar.

The application window is sometimes called the parent window, *and the document window that's contained within it is called the* child window.

Notice that, once you've opened a group, there are two windows on your screen, and thus two title bars, two Maximize buttons, two Minimize buttons, and so forth, as Figure 1.5 illustrates.

Before clicking a Minimize, Maximize, or Control-Menu button, take a quick look at the title bar that's next to the button to make sure the mouse pointer is on the correct window.

Now, for a little practice in working with an open group window:

1. Move the mouse pointer to the title bar for the Accessories window.

2. Hold down the mouse button, and drag the window to the left. Notice that you cannot move the window outside its parent application window. (Release the mouse button.)

3. Click the Maximize button on the Accessories group window.

FIGURE 1.5:

Each window has its own buttons, title bar, and borders.

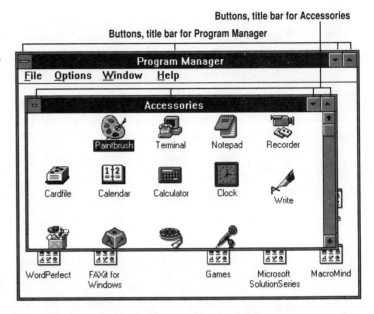

Notice that rather than expanding to full-screen size, the window fills only its parent window instead. Also, its title bar has disappeared. The name Accessories appears in the title bar for the Program Manager, and the Control-Menu box and Restore button for the Accessories window are now within the menu bar, as Figure 1.6 shows.

Now get the Accessories window back to its previous size:

FIGURE 1.6:

When you maximize a document window, such as Accessories, it expands to fill its parent window, rather than the entire screen.

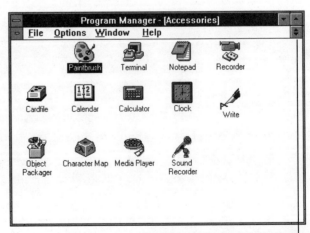

♦ Click the Accessories window's Restore button.

> *If you can't see the buttons in a group window, just drag the group window by its title bar to the left or right to bring the buttons into view.*

CLOSING A GROUP WINDOW

To close a group window, such as Accessories, thereby shrinking it back to an icon, go ahead and:

♦ Click the Minimize button on the Accessories window (*not* the Minimize button on the Program Manager window).

ABOUT THE CONTROL MENU

The upper left corner of every window also includes a Control-Menu box, which provides alternative techniques for common windowing operations. For instance, Figure 1.7 shows how the Program Manager looks after you click its Control-Menu box.

The Restore, Minimize, and Maximize options have the same effect as the equivalent buttons, and the Close option is equivalent to **File ➤ Exit**. Move and Size allow you to use the arrow keys to move or size the window; see Control Menu in the Reference section for these operations.

GETTING HELP

One of the best features of Windows is the ability to get help right when you need it, using any one of these methods:

♦ Press the Help key (**F1**).

♦ Or choose **Help ➤ Contents** from the menus (if available).

♦ Or click the Help button (if one is available).

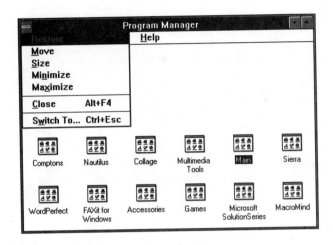

FIGURE 1.7:

Control menus offer alternative techniques for moving, sizing, and closing windows.

The help will be *context-sensitive*, meaning that it's relevant to the application window you're in at the moment. To try out the help system now:

1. Choose **Help ➤ Contents** from the Program Manager menu bar, or just press Help (**F1**) to activate help from wherever you happen to be at the moment. You'll get to a help window.

2. To get to the basic help screen for using the help system, choose **Help ➤ How to Use Help**, or press Help (**F1**) a second time. You should now see the Help screen shown in Figure 1.8.

Typically, a help window will contain more topics than can fit within the window. But you can use the scroll bar at the right of the help window, as well as the ↑, ↓, PgUp, and PgDn keys to scroll through available topics. And of course, you can size and move the help window just like any other window.

TIP

*If you'd like to keep the help window in view while you do other things, choose **Help ➤ Always on Top** from the Help window's menu bar. Choose those options a second time to disable the Always On Top option.*

Within the help window, you can click on a *jump* (any underlined topic) to get help with that topic. You can also click on any term that's underlined with dots for a

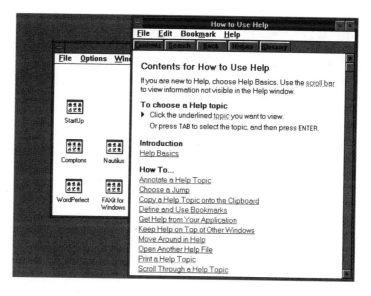

FIGURE 1.8:

The How to Use Help window provides general information for using the Windows help system.

quick definition of that term. (Clicking the mouse button a second time will remove the definition.)

Perhaps the best way to learn about help is to use it. Feel free to click any jump to get more information on any topic of your choosing.

EXITING HELP

When you want to exit help:

- Double-click the Control-Menu box in the upper left corner of the How To Use Help window (*not* the Program Manager window.), or choose File ➤ Exit from the Help window's menu bar.

If you minimize the Help window, it's reduced to a "question mark" icon near the lower left corner of the screen (or desktop, as it's called in Windows). Double-click that icon to reopen the Help window.

REINFORCING WHAT YOU'VE JUST LEARNED

Windows offers two convenient and enjoyable ways to practice and reinforce the skills you've just learned:

- To run the Windows tutorial, choose **Help ➤ Windows Tutorial** from the Program Manager's menu bar. The tutorial is self-explanatory, so just follow the instructions on the screen.

- Try a game of Windows Solitaire, by double-clicking its icon in the Games window.

Both applications can give you plenty of practice in moving and sizing windows, maximizing, minimizing, and restoring them, and selecting from menus.

MORE TIDYING UP

If you want to rearrange your icons now, choose **Window ➤ Arrange Icons** again. But this time, if you don't like the way Windows has arranged the icons, try swapping a few:

- Drag one icon until it's partly overlapping another, and drag the second icon back where the first was. Choose **Window ➤ Arrange Icons** again to fine-tune the placement, and repeat the process until you are satisfied with the arrangement.

SAVING THE PROGRAM MANAGER'S APPEARANCE

Once you're satisfied with the Program Manager window's size, position, and arrangement of icons, you can save that arrangement so that future Windows sessions start with the screen looking that way. Here's how:

1. Hold down the Shift key.

2. Choose **File ➤ Exit Windows** from the Program Manager menu bar.

3. Release the Shift key.

Not much will seem to happen, but rest assured that the next time you start Windows, your screen will look just the way it does right now.

Selecting the **Options ➤ Save Settings on Exit** *command tells Windows always to save the current arrangement of windows and icons for your next Windows session.*

EXITING WINDOWS

It's always a good idea to exit Windows before turning off your computer, to ensure that any work you've done while in Windows will be saved. To exit Windows:

1. Double-click the Program Manager Control-Menu box, or choose **File ➤ Exit Windows** from its menu bar. You'll see the *dialog box* shown in Figure 1.9.

FIGURE 1.9:
This message warns you when you're about to leave Windows and return to DOS. If you get here by accident, choose Cancel or press Escape.

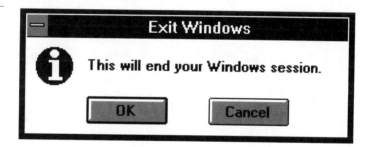

2. If you're sure you're ready to exit Windows, choose OK by clicking that button or pressing ↵.

If you'd left any unsaved work behind, Windows would ask whether to save that work. Choose whatever option is appropriate. You'll be returned to the DOS command prompt, with all your work saved. This is the "safe" time to turn off your computer.

THE BIGGER PICTURE

In most Windows applications, the term *document window* refers to any text or graphics (or both) that you're creating or editing within that application. For instance, in Figure 1.10, WordPerfect for Windows is the only open application on the desktop. The FAX cover sheet shows sample WordPerfect text in an open WordPerfect document window. Two other WordPerfect document windows are currently minimized; their icons are within the WordPerfect application window. Other applications are currently minimized, and appear near the bottom of the Windows desktop.

One of the beauties of Windows is that you can arrange windows and icons on-the-fly, in whatever fashion is convenient at the moment. To move an icon, just drag it to its new location.

· **FIGURE 1.10:**
· In this example,
· WordPerfect for
· Windows appears in
an open application
window, and a FAX
cover sheet appears
within an open
WordPerfect
document window.
All other windows
are currently
minimized to icons.

Open application window (WordPerfect)

Open document window (WordPerfect document)

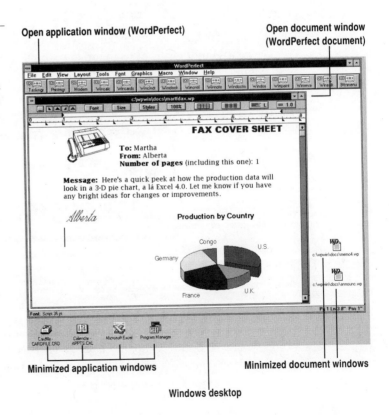

Minimized application windows

Minimized document windows

Windows desktop

FOR MORE INFORMATION

To learn more about the techniques presented in this lesson, see the following entries in the Reference section of this book:

Control Menu

Help

Icons

Menus

RUNNING
APPLICATIONS

Windows' main job is to provide a means of running other application programs, and for that reason the Program Manager is typically the first application window you see when you start Windows. When you first install Windows, the applications that came with your Windows program are stored in three groups, named Main, Accessories, and Games. There's also a group called Startup which, as you'll learn in Lesson 9, lets you "autostart" certain applications whenever you start Windows.

Your Program Manager window might also contain several other groups, each with icons for starting additional applications you've purchased and installed separately. For instance, Figure 2.1 shows a Program Manager window with quite a few applications installed.

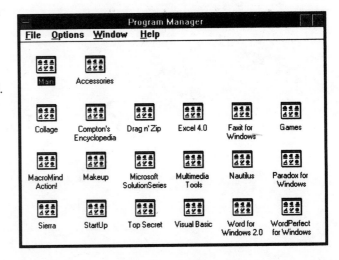

For the most part, we'll stick to applications that came with your Windows program in these lessons, so you can always follow along with your mouse and keyboard. But keep in mind that most of the techniques you'll learn here will work with virtually any Windows application you run.

RUNNING APPLICATIONS

Running an application that's already included in the Program Manager is a simple two-step process:

1. Open the group that contains the application you want to run.

2. Double-click the application's icon.

Let's give it a whirl by running the Clock application in the Accessories group:

1. If you exited Windows in the previous lesson, get it started again by typing **win** and pressing ↵ at the DOS command prompt.

2. Double-click the Accessories group icon to open that group.

3. If you can't see the Clock's application icon, first choose **Window ➤ Arrange Icons** to tidy up the icons in that group. Then, if necessary, you can increase the size of the Accessories window, or use the scroll bars on the window to scroll the Clock icon into view.

4. Double-click the Clock icon.

To "run," "start," and "launch" an application all mean the same thing—to bring a copy of the application into memory (RAM) and onto the screen. An "open" or "running" application is one that is on the screen and ready for use. An application that you've started and then minimized is still open until you explicitly close it (as discussed later in this lesson).

The Clock application starts up, as in Figure 2.2. If yours doesn't look quite like the one in the figure (perhaps because you share your computer with another user), you can easily change it using the following techniques:

♦ If Clock appears in full-screen mode, click its Restore button in the upper right corner of the Clock window.

♦ If Clock appears as a small icon in the lower left corner of the desktop, double-click that icon.

♦ If your clock is in digital format, and you want it to look like ours, choose **Settings ➤ Analog** from the Clock window's title bar.

♦ If the date or time is wrong, don't worry. You'll learn how to correct that in Lesson 3.

♦ Remember, you can move and size the Clock window just as you would any other.

Remember that even if you can't see a particular window at the moment because it happens to be covered by some other window, the covered window is still on the desktop.

FIGURE 2.2:

The Clock application is open on the desktop, and partially overlaps the Program Manager window.

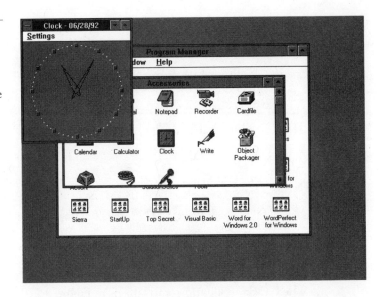

One of the first things you'll notice is that Clock probably covers all or part of Program Manager. This often happens in Windows, and it can drive ex-DOS users crazy. How, if one window is covering another, do you get back to the window that's *under* the one on top? Well, there are lots of ways to do that, as you'll learn next.

CHOOSING A WINDOW

When two or more windows are on the screen, only one window is the *active window*. You can tell which open window is active in two ways: 1) it's in the foreground, and 2) its title bar is darker or brighter (depending on your color scheme) than title bars on the inactive windows. In Figure 2.2, the Clock window is active.

Here's a quick rundown of the various techniques you can use to make any window on your desktop currently active:

- ◆ Click any visible portion of the window that you want to bring to the forefront (if possible).

- ◆ Or, hold down the Alt key and press Tab until the name of the window you want to open appears in the box at the center of the screen. Then release the Alt key.

- ◆ Or, minimize any window that's in the way by clicking its Minimize button (optionally, you can close the window, as described a little later).

- ◆ Or, double-click any "neutral" area of the desktop (where there is no window), or press Ctrl+Esc to bring up the Task List. Then double-click the name of the window you want to bring to the forefront (or highlight its name and press ↵).

To try the first three methods, follow these steps:

1. Click the title bar (or any other visible portion) of the Program Manager window. That window comes to the foreground.

2. To make Clock the active window again, using the second technique, hold down the Alt key and press Tab. You'll see a box in the center of the screen identifying Clock as the next window. Just release the Alt key to make it the active window.

3. To move Clock out of the way, click its Minimize button. Now you can see the entire Program Manager, and Clock is currently minimized as an icon, as in Figure 2.3.

FIGURE 2.3:

Clock is minimized and now appears as an icon in the lower left corner of the desktop.

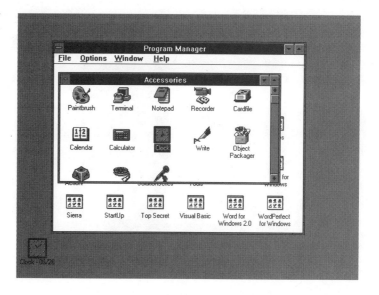

RUNNING LOTS OF APPLICATIONS

As you gain experience with Windows, you'll probably open numerous applications from time to time. To get some practice in managing lots of windows, let's clutter up the desktop with several applications. (You'll learn how to use these applications in upcoming lessons.) Follow these steps:

1. Double-click the Paintbrush icon in the Accessories group to run that application.

2. Press Alt+Tab to return to Program Manager.

3. Double-click the Cardfile (or Index Card Handler) icon.

4. Press Alt+Tab to return to Program Manager.

5. Double-click the Calendar icon.

Now you've opened several applications, and each is in its own window. Here you can see that the windows really overlap one another, as Figure 2.4 shows (your screen might look different).

FIGURE 2.4:

When several windows are open on the desktop, they will probably overlap one another.

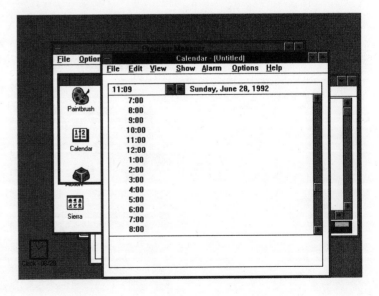

RUMMAGING THROUGH OPEN APPLICATIONS

With so many open windows on the screen, it may be difficult to click on a part of the window that you want to bring to the forefront. Here's where the Alt+Tab key really comes in handy:

1. Hold down the Alt key.

2. Press and release Tab repeatedly. Notice that pressing Tab while the Alt key is held down cycles through all your open applications, showing the name of an application in the center of the screen, as in Figure 2.5.

FIGURE 2.5:
Alt-Tab cycles through open applications.

3. Release the Alt key when the name of the application that you want to bring to the forefront appears (choose any application you want).

USING TASK LIST TO CHOOSE AN APPLICATION

TIP

Both Alt+Tab and Task List are excellent tools for taking a quick inventory of what's on your desktop at the moment.

Another handy tool for managing multiple application windows is Task List. To open Task List:

1. Double-click any visible portion of the desktop that isn't covered by a window, or press Ctrl+Esc. The Task List appears, as in Figure 2.6. The names you see in the list represent applications that are currently open on the desktop.

2. Double-click the name of the application you want to switch to (Program Manager might be a good candidate right now).

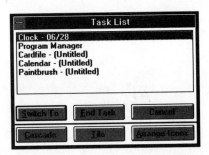

FIGURE 2.6:

Task List pops up whenever you double-click some neutral area of the desktop, or press Ctrl+Esc. It includes a list of all currently open applications.

Once you've chosen an application from the Task List, that application comes to the forefront, and Task List politely disappears from the screen.

TILING AND CASCADING APPLICATION WINDOWS

In addition to letting you choose any open application to bring to the forefront, Task List also lets you rearrange all your application windows in either Tiled or Cascading formats. To try it out:

1. Call up Task List, either by double-clicking the desktop, or by pressing Ctrl+Esc.

2. Choose Tile (by clicking that button or by pressing Alt+T). The various windows are now tiled on the screen, as in Figure 2.7.

> The minimized Clock application will stay minimized. Only the open application windows will be tiled.

FIGURE 2.7:

Multiple windows tiled on the screen, after calling up the Task List and choosing the Tile button.

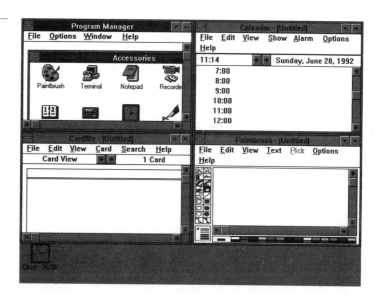

3. To cascade the windows, first call up the Task List again.

4. Choose Cascade by clicking that button or by pressing Alt+C.

Now the windows are neatly stacked on the desktop, and you can see at least some portion of each application's window (Figure 2.8). To choose a particular window to bring to the forefront, just click its title bar or any other visible portion.

> *To tile or cascade the* document *windows with an application window, choose* **Window** ➤ **Tile** *or* **Window** ➤ **Cascade** *from the application's menu bar.*

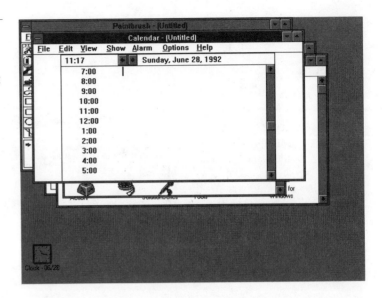

FIGURE 2.8:

Multiple windows stacked on the desktop in cascading format.

Keep in mind that once you've chosen a window, you can use the techniques described earlier to move that window to a more convenient location and size it to your liking.

CLOSING (EXITING) APPLICATIONS

Knowing how to exit (close) an application is just as important as knowing how to start it, because you never want to turn off your computer until all your applications are closed. Doing so would very likely lead to lost data and corrupted files.

A "closed" application is one that's on disk, but not currently in memory nor on the screen.

There are several ways to close applications, and you can use whichever is most convenient for you. Here they are in a nutshell (but don't try any of these techniques just yet):

- Double-click the application's Control-Menu box,
- Or, choose **File ➤ Exit** from the application's menu bar,

- Or, press Alt+F4.

- Or, if the application is currently reduced to an icon on the desktop, click the icon once to view its Control menu. Then choose **Close** to close that application.

When you have done any unsaved work in the application you're closing, you'll be asked if you want to save that work. Usually, you'll want to choose Yes, unless you're certain you want to "trash" whatever work you've been doing.

Keep in mind that closing Program Manager's window will exit Windows and return you to DOS. You'll first see the warning shown in Figure 1.9 in the previous lesson. So, if you got there by accident, and don't want to exit Windows, just choose Cancel or press Escape.

Let's close some application windows now, by following these steps:

1. First, just to play it safe, let's minimize (not close) Program Manager's window. If necessary, use Alt+Tab to bring this window forward.

2. Click Program Manager's Minimize button. That entire window is reduced to an icon.

3. Double-click the Control-Menu box on the Calendar window (or whichever window happens to be active).

4. Now double-click the Control-Menu box on the Cardfile window (or whichever window happens to be in the forefront).

5. To try the menu technique, choose **File ➤ Exit** from Paintbrush's menu bar (or whatever application happens to be left on your screen).

TIP

If you can't see the Control-Menu bar for a particular window, press Alt+Tab until you see that window's title. When you release the Alt key, you'll be able to see the entire window.

Now you're left with two minimized icons—one for Clock and another for Program Manager. Here's a shortcut for closing an application that's currently minimized:

1. Click (once) on the Clock icon.

2. From the Control menu that appears, choose **Close**.

3. Now reopen Program Manager's window by double-clicking it (or by clicking it once and choosing **Restore** from the Control menu).

Your Program Manager reappears on the screen, with the Accessories group window still open. To close that group window:

1. Press Ctrl+F4 or click the Minimize button in the Accessories window's title bar.

2. If you need to tidy up your icons now, choose **Window ➤ Arrange Icons**.

If you prefer using the keyboard to using the mouse, keep in mind that you press Ctrl+F4 to close a document window, Alt+F4 to close an application window.

So now you're back to a "clean slate" with just your Program Manager window open, with its various group icons minimized within it.

THE BIGGER PICTURE

The techniques you've learned in this lesson all work fine for running programs that are already installed in Windows and are contained in some group in the Program Manager. But you will probably install new Windows applications, and you probably have DOS applications that you still want to run. How can you run those programs?

RUNNING NEW WINDOWS APPLICATIONS

When you install a new Windows application (according to its manufacturer's instructions), you'll be instructed to run either Windows Setup or the application's own setup program. This procedure will create a Program Manager icon and a group window from which you can run the application, and it will provide Windows with all the information it needs to run the application efficiently. See Windows Setup in the Reference.

RUNNING DOS APPLICATIONS

After installing Windows, you can continue to run DOS applications from the DOS prompt. But sooner or later you'll want the convenience of running these programs from Windows.

When you first installed Windows, it may have automatically added to the Program Manager some icons for your DOS applications. You can run any of those applications in the usual way. Unfortunately, Windows does this automatic setup for only a few of the most popular DOS programs. If one of your DOS applications doesn't have an icon, you have several ways to run it from Windows:

- Start it from File Manager, as described in Lesson 8.

- Choose **File ➤ Run** and enter the program's complete path name (for example, WordPerfect 5.1 for DOS might be stored as **C:\wp51\wp.exe**).

- Set up an icon for the program, as described under DOS Applications in the Reference. (In doing so, you'll create a Program Information File (PIF) for the application; see PIF Editor in the Reference for more information about such files.) Although this method is more work initially, it's the most reliable and in the long run the most convenient.

Regardless of how you start a DOS application from Windows, that application will most likely fill the screen in the usual manner for DOS programs. But Windows is still active and running behind the scenes. You have several ways to get back to Windows *without* closing the DOS application:

- Press Alt+↵ to reduce the DOS application to a window. You may see a message indicating that the application can't be used in this "windowed" state. Choose OK to proceed anyway.

If you're running Windows in Standard mode, rather than 386 Enhanced mode, you won't be able to shrink a DOS application to a window.

- To return a windowed DOS application to full-screen size and normal functionality, press Alt+↵ again.

♦ To switch from the DOS application to another application, hold down Alt and press Tab repeatedly. Release the Alt key when the name of the application you want appears.

CLOSING DOS APPLICATIONS

Closing DOS applications is not quite as simple as closing Windows applications, mainly because DOS applications don't follow any Common User Access guidelines. Nonetheless, you need to try and close a DOS application before exiting Windows, or you'll get an error message. Here are some tips for closing a DOS application from Windows:

♦ If the DOS application is currently in a windowed state, you must return it to full-screen state, by making sure its window is the active window, then pressing Alt+↵.

♦ Use the application's normal exit procedure to close it—for example, Exit (F7) in WordPerfect, /QY in Lotus 1-2-3. You'll be returned to the Program Manager window.

Choosing **File ➤ Exit** *from the menu bar is a common technique for exiting both Windows and DOS applications correctly.*

♦ If you get stuck in a DOS application that you don't know how to exit, first reduce that application to a window by pressing Alt+↵. Then click the window's Control-Menu box, and choose **Settings** from the menu. Then click the Terminate button, read the warning, and choose OK.

♦ If you *really* get stuck in a DOS application (the screen doesn't respond to the mouse or keyboard at all), and all else fails, press Ctrl+Alt+Del. You'll see some instructions and options for closing the application as gracefully as possible.

FOR MORE INFORMATION

For more information on running applications from the Windows Program Manager, see the following Reference entries:

DOS Applications

Drives, Directories, and Files

Icons

PIF Editor

PERSONALIZING YOUR DESKTOP

After you've learned your way around the Windows desktop, and gotten a feel for opening and closing applications, you might want to personalize your desktop a bit. For instance, you might want to choose different screen colors. Or, if you've installed an optional sound card, you might want to replace the dull beep you hear from time to time with a more exciting sound. First, of course, you'll need to get Windows up and running again if you exited back to DOS in the previous lesson.

ABOUT DIALOG BOXES

Many of the features we'll describe in this lesson require that you respond to options in *dialog boxes*, a fundamental component of the Windows interface. The skills you develop working with dialog boxes here will serve you in any Windows application you may run. Figure 3.1 shows a sample dialog box, with the various types of options you're likely to come across.

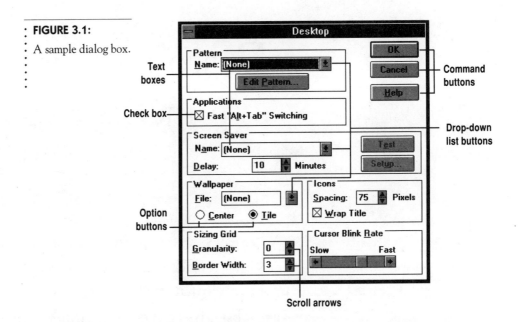

FIGURE 3.1:

A sample dialog box.

As you'll learn in this lesson, indicating your choices with these dialog box components is simply a matter of clicking the mouse (or sometimes scrolling and clicking). But if you want a more general overview of using dialog boxes before you proceed, or want to learn alternative keyboard techniques, see Dialog Boxes in the Reference.

GETTING TO THE CONTROL PANEL

You'll use the Control Panel window for most of the exercises in this lesson. To get to the Control Panel:

1. Open the Main group by double-clicking its icon.

2. Double-click the Control Panel icon. The Control Panel window appears, as shown in Figure 3.2.

FIGURE 3.2:

The Control Panel includes several accessories for personalizing Windows.

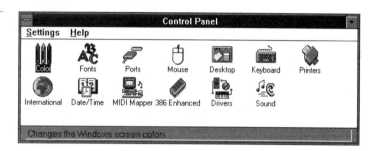

We'll just leave Control Panel on the desktop for a while now, since you'll be using a few of its features in this lesson.

CHANGING THE SCREEN COLORS

One of the first things you might want to do when personalizing Windows is to choose a color scheme that looks good on your particular monitor. Here's how:

1. In Control Panel, double-click the Color icon to get to the Color dialog box, shown in Figure 3.3.

2. Click the drop-down list button next to the name of the current color scheme to view a list of available color schemes.

3. Use the mouse or the ↑ and ↓ keys to scroll through the various color schemes. The Sample Screen in the middle of the dialog box shows an example of the currently selected color scheme.

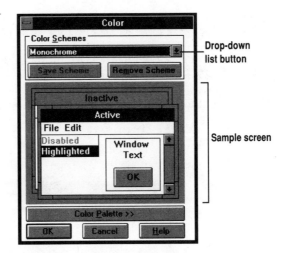

FIGURE 3.3:
The Color dialog
box lets you choose
a color scheme for
Windows.

The menus and buttons in the Sample Screen don't do anything—they're just there to show how your selected color scheme will look.

4. Click the OK button after you've found a color scheme you like.

Now let's look at some more things you can do with the desktop.

CHANGING THE WALLPAPER

You can decorate your desktop with a *wallpaper* picture or pattern. Windows 3.1 comes with several wallpaper pictures that you can try out. Let's give it a whirl:

1. Double-click the Desktop icon in the Control Panel window. You'll see the Desktop dialog box (Figure 3.4).

2. Click the drop-down list button next to File: in the Wallpaper area of the dialog box. You'll see a list of available wallpapers, as shown in Figure 3.4 (your wallpaper collection might be different).

3. Scroll through the list as you did with the color schemes. To choose a wallpaper, click its name once.

FIGURE 3.4:

Available wallpapers, made visible by opening the drop-down list in the Wallpaper area of the Desktop dialog box.

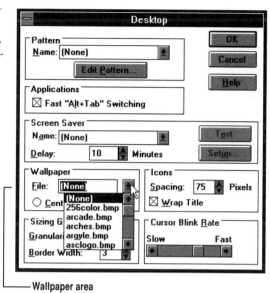

Wallpaper area

4. Tile and Center are *radio* buttons, so called because only one can be selected at a time. Clicking one option "deselects" the other. For most wallpapers, click the Tile option. Use the Center option only for full-screen images.

5. Click the OK button.

6. To see all of the wallpaper, as in Figure 3.5 (which displays the win-logo.bmp wallpaper, tiled), minimize both the Control Panel and Program Manager windows.

7. To try different wallpapers, double-click the Control Panel icon and repeat steps 1 through 6 as needed.

TIP

You can use virtually any picture—a family photo, company logo, your signature, personal artwork—whatever, for the wallpaper, as described near the end of this lesson.

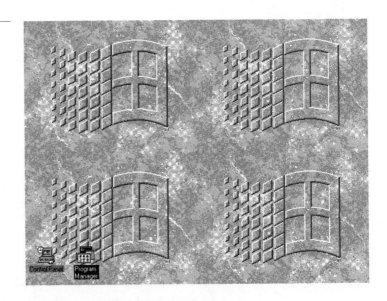

FIGURE 3.5:
After choosing the winlogo.bmp wallpaper, your desktop will look more like this.

THE DOWN-SIDE TO USING WALLPAPER

A couple of disadvantages to using a fancy bit map image for your wallpaper are that 1) the wallpaper takes up memory and 2) the time it takes to redraw the wallpaper can slow down Windows performance considerably. If you find that Windows is running too slowly, or you get "out of memory" errors after choosing a wallpaper, you can get rid of the wallpaper by repeating the above steps, and choosing **(None)** from the list in Step 3.

CHOOSING A SCREEN SAVER

If the same image is left on your screen for too long, it may be "burned into" the screen, leading to eventual blurring. A *screen saver* is an application that prevents burn-in by moving some image around on your screen after the computer has been idle for a few minutes. To choose a screen saver:

1. If necessary, reopen the Control Panel and double-click the Desktop icon to return to the Desktop dialog box.

2. Click the drop-down list button next to Name in the Screen Saver area of the Desktop dialog box. You'll see a list of available Screen Savers, something like Figure 3.6.

3. Click (once) the name of any screen saver.

4. To see how your selected screen saver will look, click the Test button. Moving the mouse (even slightly) will end the test and return you to the dialog box.

TIP
The Microsoft Entertainment Pack includes Idle Wild—additional screen savers you can use with Windows 3.1.

5. Repeat steps 2 through 4 until you find a screen saver that you like.

6. In the box next to Delay, specify the number of minutes you want the computer to be idle before the screen saver begins. You can click the small scroll arrows to the right of the box to increase or decrease this amount (5 or 10 minutes is a reasonable setting). Scroll arrows are used in many Windows contexts, as they are here, to take you through a range of numeric values.

FIGURE 3.6:

A list of available screen savers appears when you click the drop-down list box in the Screen Saver portion of the Desktop dialog box.

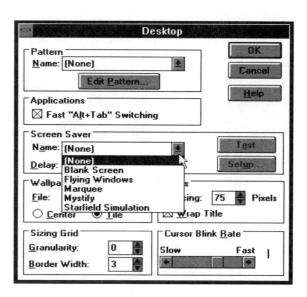

7. Choose the OK button when you're satisfied with your screen saver selection.

Remember, your screen saver won't kick in until the computer has been idle (no keyboard or mouse activity) for the delay you've specified. After it starts, simply moving the mouse or pressing any key will remove the screen saver and return you to wherever you left off.

SETTING THE CORRECT DATE AND TIME

As you saw in the previous lesson, the Clock application displays the current system date and time. If the clock is wrong, or to change between Daylight Savings and Standard time, you'll need to adjust your computer's date and time:

1. In Control Panel, double-click Date/Time. You'll see the dialog box shown in Figure 3.7.

2. Click any number you need to change, then click the up or down arrow to increase or decrease that number (or press Delete, and type in a new number). Be sure to set the AM/PM option next to the time correctly.

3. Choose OK after setting the correct date and time.

The Appointment Calendar, described in the next lesson, also uses the system date and time to sound an alarm when an appointment time arrives.

· **FIGURE 3.7:**

· The Date & Time
· dialog box lets you set
· the computer's date
· and time.

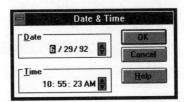

ASSIGNING CUSTOM SOUNDS TO EVENTS

If you have installed a sound card in your computer (and installed the Windows driver program for it), you can assign custom sounds to various events that occur in Windows. Here's how:

1. In the Control Panel, double-click the Sound icon. You'll see the dialog box shown in Figure 3.8 (though the exact list of sounds available to you might be different).

2. Make sure the **Enable System Sounds** check box is selected. If it isn't, click the check box until an X appears.

3. Click the event to which you want to assign a sound in the Events list box. For instance, **Asterisk** for a message displayed with an asterisk, **Default Beep** for the "regular" beep, or **Windows Start** to hear the sound as soon as you start Windows.

The volume of the sound you're testing is determined by the software for your sound card and the volume setting on the speakers (if any).

FIGURE 3.8:

The Sound dialog box lets you assign sounds to events in Windows 3.1 if you've installed a sound card (and its driver).

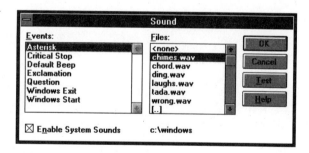

4. To test a sound, double-click the name of a sound file, or click the name once and then click the Test button. Optionally, you can switch to another drive and directory if you have additional sounds stored elsewhere (see Drives, Directories, and Files in the Reference).

5. Once you find a sound you like, leave both the event and the sound file name highlighted. Then, you can repeat steps 3 through 5 to assign sounds to other events if you wish.

6. When you've finished making your selections, choose OK.

You won't hear the sound until its event occurs. For instance, if you assigned a sound to Windows Exit, you'll hear that sound next time you exit Windows to return to DOS.

RETURNING TO PROGRAM MANAGER

Let's work our way back to Program Manager now, where we can take a break (and consider further sources of wallpaper) before moving on to the next lesson:

1. Close Control Panel by double-clicking its Control-Menu box, or by choosing **Settings ➤ Exit**.

2. If Program Manager is still minimized, double-click its icon to restore it.

3. If the Main window is still open, click its Minimize button.

If you're ready to call it a day, now would be a good time to exit Windows. (Remember how? Just choose **File ➤ Exit** from the menu bar.)

THE BIGGER PICTURE

As mentioned, you can use any printed material as your Windows wallpaper. Figure 3.9 shows a scanned photograph used as wallpaper.

To create your own wallpaper from a printed document, you'll need access to a scanner that can save images in one of the formats that the Windows 3.1 wallpaper supports: Windows bit map (.bmp), device-independent bit map (.dib), and Run-Length Encoded (.rle). If you don't have a scanner of your own, check

FIGURE 3.9:

Scanned photo used as wallpaper.

with local print shops and desktop publishing services to see if they can scan the image for you.

Any drawing you create with Windows Paintbrush (see Lesson 6) will be saved as a .bmp file, and Windows will automatically add it to the list of files available as wallpapers.

If you want the wallpaper to fill the screen, you'll need to scale, and possibly crop, the image as it's being scanned to the pixel dimensions of your monitor (see Table 3.1). This is simple to do with most scanner software.

Once you've created the scanned file, just copy it to your Windows directory. Then you'll be able to select that file from the list of wallpapers. Also, as you'll see in Lesson 6, you'll be able to use that picture in any written document.

TABLE 3.1: Pixel Dimensions of Various Display Types

DISPLAY TYPE	PIXELS (WIDTH × HEIGHT)
VGA	640 × 480
Super VGA	800 × 600
XGA and others	1024 × 768

FOR MORE INFORMATION

For more information on personalizing Windows, and other topics introduced in this chapter, see the following Reference entries:

Date/Time

Dialog Boxes

Drives, Directories, and Files

Screen Saver

Sound

HANDY APPLETS
FOR GETTING
ORGANIZED

The Accessories group offers the *standard applications* that came with your Windows 3.1 program. These applications are often called *applets*, because they're small, easy to learn, and easy to use. But best of all, they're very handy, so you may find yourself using them every day.

And like the Control Panel in Lesson 3, these applets present essentially the same interface as more sophisticated Windows programs you may run; the practice you get here in saving, opening, and printing files will make learning those programs easier.

CREATING AN ELECTRONIC ROLODEX

Cardfile is a handy applet that you can use as an electronic business card file. To open Cardfile:

1. Open the Accessories group by double-clicking its icon as usual.

2. Double-click the Cardfile icon (which might also be titled Index Card Handler). Cardfile initially appears with an empty index card, as shown in Figure 4.1.

Notice that the title bar indicates that you're currently working with an Untitled set of cards. This just means that your current card file is empty. You'll learn how to create, save, and open card files in a moment.

FIGURE 4.1:

The Cardfile applet with an empty index card in view.

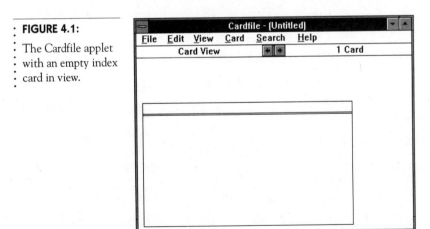

As with any window, you can move Cardfile to a more convenient location, if you wish, by dragging its title bar. Or you can change its size by dragging one of its borders (though you can't change the size of the cards within the window).

ADDING AN INDEX CARD

The first thing you'll want to do after starting Cardfile for the first time is create an index card. Take the following steps:

1. Choose **Card ➤ Add**.

2. In the Add dialog box that appears, type the index line entry. The cards will be alphabetized by this entry, so type the entry as you'd like it to be filed; for instance, **Smith, Joan**.

3. Choose OK.

4. Fill in the rest of the index card as you wish, keeping in mind a few pointers:

   ◆ Press ↵ after typing each line. You can use the Backspace and Delete keys, and cut-and-paste techniques (Lesson 5) to delete, copy, and move text.

TIP

If you have a Hayes or Hayes-compatible modem installed on your computer and connected to your telephone, you can have Cardfile automatically dial the phone number on the current card. See Cardfile in the Reference for details.

   ◆ If you plan to use the automatic dialing feature, make the phone number the first entry under the index line. Include all the numbers to be dialed.

   ◆ Type the name and address in the standard format used for addressing letters and envelopes. That way, you can easily cut-and-paste that information to a letter or envelope later.

   ◆ You can add any "keywords" to the card, simply by typing the appropriate word or phrase anywhere on the card. For instance, you might add the word *flowers* to a card for your florist, so that later you can tell Cardfile to "find the card with the word 'flowers' on it."

Figure 4.2 shows a sample card file with several cards added. The card in front has been filled in with name, address, and telephone number. If you want some practice now, add a few cards to your own card file by repeating steps 1 through 4 above for each card that you want to add.

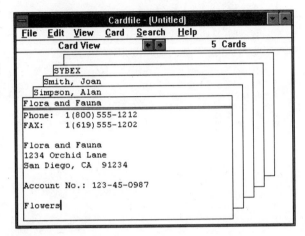

FIGURE 4.2:

A sample card file. The card in front shows a useful format to follow if you'll be using a modem to autodial phone numbers in cards.

SAVING YOUR INDEX CARDS

After you've added cards to a file, or changed existing cards, you need to save the card file. Here's how:

1. Choose **File ➤ Save** from the Cardfile menu bar. The first time you save a set of cards, you'll see the Save As dialog box, shown in Figure 4.3. The next time you save the file, it will be saved automatically with the name you give it now, and you will skip the next steps.

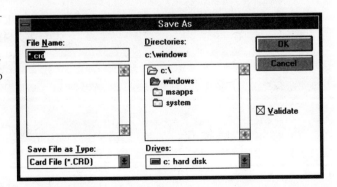

FIGURE 4.3:

The Save As dialog box lets you save any cards you've added to Cardfile, or changed recently.

2. Type a valid DOS file name (eight characters, no spaces) that will be easy to remember in the future. For instance, you might type **mycards** as your file name.

3. Choose OK. Windows will automatically add the extension .crd to whatever file name you provided.

4. If a file with the name you provided already exists, you'll see a warning to this effect. Choose No and rename the new file, or choose Yes to replace the existing file. Once you've saved your cards, the file name you gave the cards replaces Untitled in the Cardfile window's title bar during the current session.

OPENING A CARD FILE

Each time you start Cardfile, it begins with the blank Untitled window (whether you've saved one card file or several), so you need to open the file you want. Here's how:

1. Choose **File ➤ Open** from the Cardfile menu bar. The Open file dialog box appears.

2. Double-click the name of the card file you want to open.

In Lesson 9 you'll learn how to "autoload" your personal index cards, so you don't have to bother with this step in the future.

If you don't want to use one of the existing card files, just choose Cancel.

USING YOUR INDEX CARDS

Here are some basic techniques that you can use to search through, print, and change cards in your card file:

- To *scroll through* cards, click the scroll arrows on the status bar, or press the PgUp and PgDn keys.

- To bring any visible card to the front of the stack, click anywhere on the card.

- To *search* for a card, based on its index entry, choose **Search ➤ Go To** (or press F4). Then type any portion of the index entry and choose OK.

- To search for a "keyword" within a card, choose **Search ➤ Find**. Type the word or phrase you're looking for, then click the Find Next button (or press F3). Once Cardfile finds a matching card, you can click Find Next again to look for more matches or click the Cancel button to remove the Find dialog box.

Press an arrow key or click the mouse to "deselect" the matching word or phrase after a successful keyword search. If your keyword can't be found on any card, a "Cannot find…" message appears. Just click the OK button or press ↵ to remove the message.

- To *view a list* of index entries, choose **View ➤ List**. You can then highlight any entry, and choose **View ➤ Card** to view that index card.

- To *print* the current card, choose **File ➤ Print**.

- To *print all the cards*, choose **File ➤ Print All**.

- To *change* the text on the current card, simply click wherever you want to make the change. To edit the index entry, choose **Edit ➤ Index.**

*If a card contains a picture, you may need to choose **Edit ➤ Text** before making changes to the text.*

- To *delete* the card in the front of the stack, choose **Card ➤ Delete**, then choose OK.

- To *duplicate* the current card, choose **Card ➤ Duplicate**. You'll find this handy when creating a new card with some of the same information as an existing card.

CLOSING CARDFILE

You can add new cards to your card file at any time in the future, using the **Cards ➤ Add** options. For now, however, we'll close Cardfile to move on to another handy applet:

1. Double-click the Control-Menu box for Cardfile, or choose **File ➤ Exit**, to close it for the time being.

2. If you've added or changed any cards, and haven't saved those changes yet, you'll see the reminder shown in Figure 4.4. Choose Yes to ensure that your changes are saved.

FIGURE 4.4:

Message that appears when you attempt to exit Cardfile or Windows with unsaved changes in your card file.

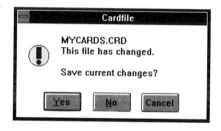

Cardfile

MYCARDS.CRD
This file has changed.

Save current changes?

Yes   No   Cancel

TIP

If you minimize, rather than close, Cardfile you won't need to use **File ➤ Open** *again during the current session to reopen your cards.*

KEEPING YOUR APPOINTMENTS

Another handy applet is the appointment calendar, which acts as a sort of electronic Day-Timer, with the added bonus of sounding an alarm as an appointment time draws near. To open Calendar:

1. If the Accessories window isn't already open, double-click its icon.

2. Double-click the Calendar icon. The Calendar appears, as in Figure 4.5.

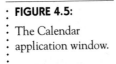

FIGURE 4.5:

The Calendar
application window.

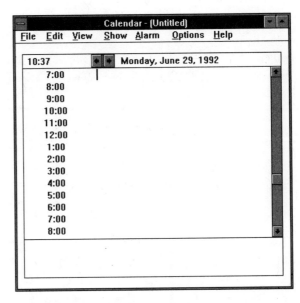

The first thing you might want to do is make sure that the current date and time in the status bar are correct. If they aren't, you'll want to reset your computer's date and time, as described in Lesson 3.

CHOOSING A CALENDAR VIEW

Before you begin entering appointments and saving them as a file, it will be helpful to familiarize yourself with the two ways you can view the Calendar, *Day view* (shown in Figure 4.5), and *Month view*, shown in Figure 4.6.

To switch from one view to the other:

- Choose **View** and then the view you want,

- Or press F8 for Day view, or F9 for Month view,

- Or double-click the current date in the status bar,

- Or, if you're in Month view and want to view the appointments for a particular date, double-click the appropriate date.

FIGURE 4.6:

Appointment
Calendar as it appears
in Month view.

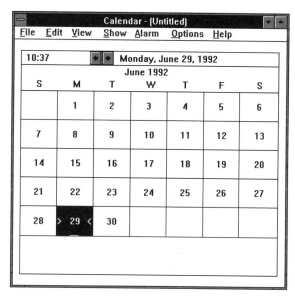

USING DAY VIEW

In Day view, you can switch to any other day to enter an appointment using any of
the following techniques:

- Click the scroll arrows in the status bar to scroll forward or backward
  through days.

- Choose **Show ➤ Next**, or press Ctrl+PgDn to see tomorrow's
  date. Choose **Show ➤ Previous**, or press Ctrl+PgUp, to see the pre-
  ceding day.

- To move to a particular date, choose **Show ➤ Date**, enter a date in
  mm/dd/yy format (for example, 12/31/92), then choose OK.

- Choose **Show ➤ Today** to see the current date.

Using Month View

You can use similar techniques in Month view to scroll around from date to date:

- Click the scroll arrows in the status bar to scroll forward a month at a time, or backward a month at a time.

- Choose **Show ➤ Next** to view the next month, or **Show ➤ Previous** to view the previous month.

- Press Ctrl+PgDn for the next month, or Ctrl+PgUp for the previous month.

- To move to a specific date, choose **Show ➤ Date**, enter a date in mm/dd/yy format (for example, 12/31/92), then choose OK.

- Choose **Show ➤ Today** to view the current month.

- Click any day in the current month to move the highlighter to that date, or double-click to switch to the Day view for that particular day.

ENTERING APPOINTMENTS

To enter an appointment into the Calendar:

1. If you're in Month view, double-click the date for the appointment. You'll be taken to Day view for that date. Starting from Day view, you can scroll to the date.

2. Click the time of the appointment (or the time that you want to be reminded of the appointment). If the appointment isn't right on the hour, choose **Options ➤ Special Time**. Type the appointment time in hh:mm format, choose AM or PM, then choose **Insert**.

4. Type the information describing the appointment, up to 80 characters.

5. If you want to set an audible alarm for the appointment, choose **Alarm ➤ Set**. A small bell appears next to the appointment, as in the example shown in Figure 4.7.

If you change your mind about the alarm, just click the time spot that you set the alarm for, and choose **Alarm ➤ Set** *again to remove the little bell.*

FIGURE 4.7:

Sample appointment with alarm set, as indicated by the small bell.

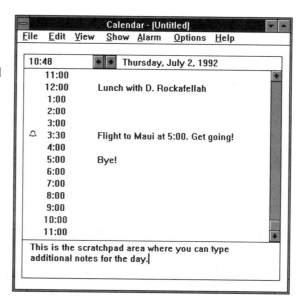

6. If you want to have the alarm go off a few minutes before the scheduled appointment time, choose **Alarm ➤ Controls**. You'll see the dialog box shown in Figure 4.8. Type a number from 0 to 10 in the Early Ring box. Make sure Sound is selected. Then click the OK button or press ↵.

FIGURE 4.8:

The Alarm Controls dialog box.

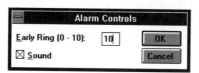

7. To add any general notes to the current appointment day, click the scratch pad beneath the last time slot, and type up to three lines of text.

SAVING APPOINTMENTS

After entering an appointment, remember to save the appointment calendar by following these steps:

1. Choose **File ➤ Save** from the Calendar menu.

2. If you've never saved the current appointment calendar, you'll see a Save As dialog box similar to the one for Cardfile. Enter a valid file name and choose OK. Windows will automatically add the extension .cal to whatever name you provide.

OPENING YOUR PERSONAL APPOINTMENT CALENDAR

Once you've saved an appointment calendar, you'll want to check your appointments from time to time. Use the same basic technique you'd use to open index cards:

1. Choose **File ➤ Open**.

2. Double-click the name of the appointment calendar to open.

PRINTING APPOINTMENTS

If you want to print your appointments at any time:

1. Choose **File ➤ Print**. You'll see the dialog box shown in Figure 4.9.

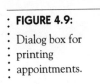

FIGURE 4.9:
Dialog box for printing appointments.

2. To print appointments starting at some date other than the date shown, type the starting date in mm/dd/yy format.

3. Press Tab, or click anywhere in the To text box, then enter an ending date in mm/dd/yy format. To print the appointments just for the From date, leave this text box empty.

4. Choose OK.

ENSURING THE ALARM WILL BE HEARD

Any alarms that you set in the appointment calendar will sound *only* if Calendar is open when the scheduled time arrives. On days for which you have any alarms set, you'll want to minimize, rather than close, Calendar.

EVER-READY CALCULATOR

Pop quiz—what's the total cost of an order for $123.45 with 7.75% sales tax, and $15.00 in shipping costs added? Cat got your brain? Let the Calculator help:

1. If it isn't already open, open the Accessories group.

2. Double-click the Calculator icon to view the calculator (Figure 4.10).

If your calculator first appears as a large scientific calculator, choose **View ▶ Standard** *from its menu bar to view the simpler calculator shown in Figure 4.10.*

You use the Windows calculator as you would any other, but you can either type numbers and arithmetic signs such as + (add), − (subtract), * (multiply), or /

FIGURE 4.10:

The calculator.

(divide), or click their equivalent buttons. For instance, to get the answer to the pop quiz, you would take the following steps:

1. Type **123.45** or click the appropriate buttons with your mouse (don't forget the decimal point).

2. Type or click *.

3. Type **1.0775.**

4. Type or click =.

5. Now to add the shipping cost, type or click+.

6. Type **15.**

7. Type (or click)=.

The numbers on your numeric keypad work only when the Num Lock key is turned on.

The result will display more decimal places of accuracy than you need, and Calculator can't round the number for you. But at least it did the hard part, and I suspect you can round the number off to the nearest penny in your head.

CLEARING THE CURRENT NUMBER

If you make a mistake, or want to start a new calculation, clear the calculator by clicking the Clear button (C), or by pressing Esc.

CLOSING CALCULATOR

When you're done with Calculator, you can either minimize or close it to get it out of the way:

- ◆ Double-click the Control-Menu box in Calculator to close it now.

THE BIGGER PICTURE

Cardfile is a handy tool for organizing any information, not just names and addresses. For instance, you can use it to organize frequently-used pieces of text (such as employee descriptions), recipes, photos, clip art, sounds—whatever. Then, when you need one of those items, you can just browse through your index cards and cut-and-paste the item you need into your application.

You'll learn more about cut-and-paste, working with pictures, and related topics in upcoming lessons.

Figure 4.11 shows an example in which a card file named BLURBS.CRD contains brief descriptions of employees. Some cards (none shown at the moment) also contain photos of employees and recordings of their voices. Below Cardfile, a Microsoft Word for Windows document contains a copy of an employee's photo and description pasted in from the cards.

One word of warning. Placing photos and other graphic images in a Cardfile eats up substantial memory and disk space. And, even if your system has plenty of memory, scrolling through pictures in Cardfile can be slow. You can speed up the scrolling part by using Cardfile's **View ➤ List** option to view only the card indexes.

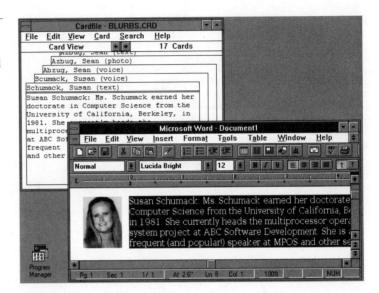

· **FIGURE 4.11:**
· Using Cardfile to
· store frequently-used
· snippets of text, clip
art, photos, and so
forth gives you a
handy way to
organize that
information, and
quick access to it as
well.

FOR MORE INFORMATION

For more information on applets, files, and other topics presented in this lesson, see:

Calendar

Cardfile

Calculator

Date/Time

Drives, Directories, and Files

Working with Text

In this lesson you'll learn some basic skills for working with text in Windows. We'll use the Write application that came with Windows 3.1 as your word processor. While not as powerful as a "full-blown" word processor, Write is handy for the occasional short document. Also, because it follows the Windows CUA (Common User Access) guidelines, most of the skills you learn here will carry over nicely to other word processors.

STARTING WRITE

To start Write (no pun intended):

1. Open the Accessories group in Program Manager.
2. Double-click the Write icon.
3. To give yourself maximum typing space, you can either enlarge the window to your liking or just click its Maximize button to expand it to full screen.

The Write application starts with a "blank sheet of paper," as in Figure 5.1. The blinking vertical bar on your screen is the *insertion point*, which shows where any new text you type will appear. Just to the right of the insertion point is the *end mark*, indicating the end of the document. The mouse pointer appears as an *I-beam* in the Write window, and it shows where the insertion point will move when you click the mouse button.

TYPING A DOCUMENT

Like all word processors, Write uses automatic word wrap, so you should press ↵ only at the end of the *paragraph*, not at the end of each line. If you want a little

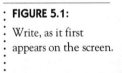

FIGURE 5.1:

Write, as it first
appears on the screen.

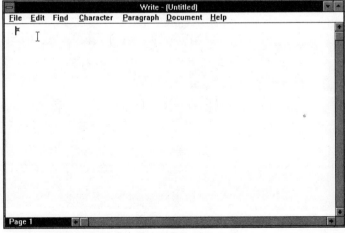

practice, you can type the sample announcement shown in Figure 5.2. Press ↵ twice after the word *Instructor* and twice more after *tenor*.

TIP

> *You may want to enlarge the Write window to near full-screen width, so you can see the entire width of your document as you type.*

FIGURE 5.2:

A sample document typed into Write.

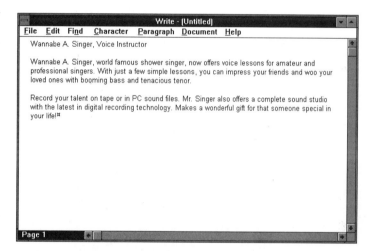

POSITIONING THE INSERTION POINT

When you want to make changes to existing text, your first task is to place the insertion point where you want to make those changes. You can use either the mouse or the keyboard:

- Use your mouse to position the I-beam where you want to move the insertion point (but not past the end mark), then click the mouse button,

- Or use the keys listed in Table 5.1 to position the insertion point.

In Table 5.1, 5 refers to the 5 key on the numeric keypad. Num Lock must be off for the 5 key to work. Keys that move from page to page work only if the document contains more than one page, *and* only after you've printed the document.

TABLE 5.11: Keys That Move the Insertion Point

TO MOVE...	PRESS
Next character	$\rightarrow$
Previous character	$\leftarrow$
Up a line	$\uparrow$
Down a line	$\downarrow$
Start of line	Home
End of line	End
Next word	Ctrl+$\rightarrow$
Previous word	Ctrl+$\leftarrow$
Next sentence	5+$\rightarrow$
Previous sentence	5+$\leftarrow$
Next paragraph	5+PgDn
Previous paragraph	5+PgUp
Next Page	5+PgDn
Previous Page	5+PgUp
Top of window	Ctrl+PgUp
Bottom of Window	Ctrl+PgDn
Top of Document	Ctrl+Home
End of Document	Ctrl+End

Also, these keys *only* move the insertion point through existing text, not past the end mark. If you're at the end of the document and want to move the insertion point to the right, use the Spacebar. To move the insertion point down, press ↵.

EDITING TEXT

Once you've placed the insertion point where you want it, you can use any of the following methods to make changes and corrections:

- To delete the character to the left of the insertion point, press Backspace. To delete the character to the right, press Delete (Del).

- To delete a blank line, move the insertion point to the beginning of that line (Home), then press Delete (Del).

- To insert a blank line above an existing one, move to the first character of that line (Home) and press ↵.

- To rejoin lines that you've accidentally broken (by pressing ↵), move to the end of the top line (press End) and press Delete.

If you made any mistakes while typing the sample letter, you may want to try out some of these techniques now to make changes and corrections.

SELECTING TEXT

Other than basic typing and editing, perhaps the most useful technique you can learn is to *select text*. Selecting text makes it possible to delete, move, and copy text within a document and from one application to another. To select text with the mouse:

1. Move the I-beam to where you want to start selecting text.

2. Hold down the mouse button and drag the I-beam through the text.

3. When you're finished selecting, release the mouse button.

TIP

In some applications (including Write), you can also use the selection area in the left margin to select blocks of text. See "Selecting Text" in the Reference for more information.

To select text using the keyboard:

1. Move the insertion point to where you want to start selecting text.
2. Hold down the Shift key, and move the insertion point with any of the keys listed in Table 5.1.
3. When you've finished selecting text, release the Shift key.

The selected text appears in reverse video. If you made a mistake and want to start over, just click the mouse button, or press any movement key without holding down the Shift key.

TIP

The selection techniques described here work in most Windows applications, and even in the small text boxes within dialog boxes.

DELETING SELECTED TEXT

To delete selected text, press the Delete key or the Backspace key. To replace it with new text, just start typing.

WARNING

If you type any regular character while text is selected, that character instantly replaces the selected text.

UNDOING YOUR MOST RECENT EDIT

If you accidentally delete or replace selected text, or make any change that you want to reverse immediately, you can choose **Edit ➤ Undo** to restore the text as it was before your most recent edit. (Then, to avoid repeating the mistake, you may want to deselect the text by pressing any arrow key or clicking the mouse button.) **Edit ➤ Undo** is available in most Windows applications and always reverses the most recent action.

MOVING AND COPYING TEXT WITH THE CLIPBOARD

You can move and copy selected text using cut-and-paste techniques based on one of Windows' most useful features, the Clipboard, which lets you move or copy text and pictures not only within a document, but even between applications. The Clipboard is a (usually invisible) "scratchpad" to which all Windows applications have access.

The basic technique for cutting and pasting is to select the text (or picture, as described in Lesson 6) that you want to move or copy. Then, if you want to copy the text, choose **Edit ➤ Copy**. Or if you want to move the text, choose **Edit ➤ Cut**. The text is copied (or moved) to the Clipboard, where it remains until you replace it with something else. Finally, move the insertion point to where you want to place the text, then choose **Edit ➤ Paste**.

To try a simple cut-and-paste operation now, you can follow these steps to move a sentence in our sample document:

1. Using either the mouse or the keyboard, move the insertion point to the beginning of the second paragraph.

2. Drag the mouse pointer to the right, or press Shift+→ (or Ctrl+→) to highlight the entire first sentence, including the blank space after the period, as shown in Figure 5.3.

FIGURE 5.3:

The first sentence in the second paragraph selected (highlighted).

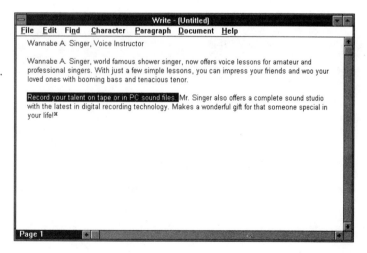

3. Choose **Edit ➤ Cut** (or press Ctrl+X) to cut that sentence to the Clipboard (it disappears from the document).

4. Place insertion point (*not* just the I-Beam) just before the sentence beginning with *Makes a wonderful gift.*

5. Choose **Edit ➤ Paste** (or press Ctrl+V).

The first sentence has now been moved to the middle of the paragraph, as Figure 5.4 shows.

If you forget to include a blank space when selecting a sentence, you can just press the Spacebar to insert one after the move. Then delete the blank space you left behind.

Many applications (but not Write) let you move selected text simply by dragging it to a new location in the document. See "Using Drag-And-Drop to Move and Copy Text" in Lesson 8.

FIGURE 5.4:

First sentence in the paragraph has been moved down in the paragraph, using cut-and-paste.

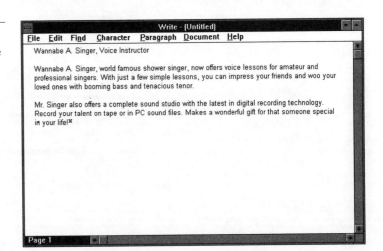

USING TRUETYPE FONTS (AND OTHERS)

Besides the fonts built into your printer (and those you may have bought and installed separately), your Windows 3.1 package comes with a set of TrueType fonts, examples of which appear in Figure 5.5. You can purchase additional TrueType fonts through Microsoft and other software vendors.

FIGURE 5.5:

Examples of the TrueType fonts that come with Windows 3.1.

Font	Example
Courier New	ABCDEFGHIJKLMnopqrstuvwxyz
Times New Roman	ABCDEFGHIJKLMnopqrstuvwxyz
Arial	ABCDEFGHIJKLMnopqrstuvwxyz
Symbol	ΑΒΧΔΕΦΓΗΙϑΚΛΜνοπθρστυϖωξψζ
Wingdings	✁✂✃✄✆✇✈✉☺☻☹✌✍■□◻◻◻◆◆❖✦⌧⌦✼

TrueType fonts offer several advantages over other fonts:

- You can use TrueType fonts with virtually any laser or dot-matrix printer, and within just about any Windows application that supports fonts.

- TrueType fonts can be scaled to any size.

- Windows uses the same typeface to print on both the screen and printer. Therefore, what you see on your screen is exactly what you'll get when printing.

- TrueType uses a new technology called *hinting*, which helps get rid of the jagged edges that some fonts show on the screen and printer.

- If you send a copy of a document with one of the default TrueType fonts to another Windows 3.1 user, that person can print the document regardless of their particular printer.

To choose a font, first move the insertion point to where you want the new font to start, or select a block of text for the new font. Then choose the options required in your application to change the font. Here are the steps you would follow in our sample Write document:

1. Move the insertion point to the top of the document by pressing Ctrl+Home.

2. Select **Wannabe A. Singer, Voice Instructor**.

3. Choose **Character ➤ Fonts**. The Font dialog box appears, as in Figure 5.6.

The exact fonts that appear in your Fonts list depend on the fonts built into your printer, as well as any you've purchased and installed. TrueType fonts are indicated by a TT symbol in the fonts list.

4. Use the scroll bars or ↑ and ↓ keys to scroll through the list of available fonts. A sample of the currently highlighted font appears in the Sample window (if you're using the scroll bar, you'll need to click a font name to see an example).

If the sample is too small to see clearly, choose a larger size from the Size list. The size of a font is measured in points, where 1 point is roughly 1/72 inch.

5. When you find a font you like, leave the highlighter on it (we'll use the Arial font in this example).

6. Now click the Font Style option. Notice that you can choose from a variety of styles (for most fonts) including Regular, *Italic*, **Bold**, and ***Bold Italic***. This example uses Regular.

FIGURE 5.6:

The Font dialog box lets you choose a font. Fonts marked with TT are TrueType fonts.

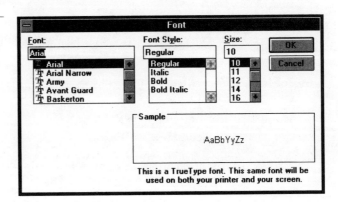

7. Click the Size box, then use the scroll bars to scroll through available sizes. For this example, you would click 20 (points).

8. Choose OK after selecting your font and size to leave the Font dialog box.

9. Click the mouse button again, or press an arrow key, to deselect the selected text.

The selected text now appears in the font and size you chose, as in Figure 5.7.

FIGURE 5.7:

The selected text now appears in Arial font, at a 20 point size.

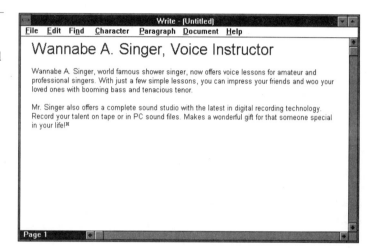

USING SPECIAL CHARACTERS

Windows offers many special characters that aren't directly available on the keyboard but can be used in just about any Windows word processor; and, in the Character Map accessory, it provides a convenient means of inserting them into your documents.

To use the Character Map, you first select the appropriate font in your word processor and place the insertion point where the character will appear. Then open the Character Map, choose the same font, and select the character you want from a grid displaying all the characters in that font (see Figure 5.8). Next, copy the character to the Clipboard, return to your word processor, and paste it into the document.

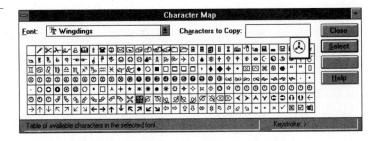

FIGURE 5.8:

Character Map lets you choose special characters to insert into your document.

To insert a logo (chosen from the TrueType Wingdings font) into the sample announcement, you would follow these steps:

1. Move the insertion point to the top of the document (press Ctrl+Home).

2. Choose **Character ➤ Fonts**. Scroll through the list and click the True-Type Wingdings font.

3. Click the Size box, and choose 72 to make the character about an inch tall.

4. Choose OK.

TIP

The inside back cover of this book lists all the Windows special characters and their keystroke equivalents. Also see Character Map in the Reference.

Now that you've chosen the font for the special character, you need to insert it:

1. Call up Task List (press Ctrl+Esc) and double-click Program Manager.

2. Double-click Character Map in the Accessories group. You should see a dialog box like the one shown in Figure 5.8.

WARNING

Character Map doesn't automatically sense what font is selected in your document (nor vice versa). So for the character to be displayed correctly in your document, you must choose the same font in both your document and the Character Map.

3. Display the drop-down list of fonts and choose TrueType Wingdings.

4. Point to the tape reel special character (second-to-last in the top row), and hold down the mouse button to magnify it and verify your selection. (In Figure 5.8, the character is already magnified.) When you release the mouse button, that character is framed.

5. Click the Select button. The framed character appears in the text box next to Characters to Copy.

6. Choose **Copy** to copy that character to the Clipboard.

7. You can now choose **Close** to close the Character Map.

TIP

When selecting quite a few special characters, you might prefer to minimize, rather than close, Character Map so it's readily available on the desktop.

8. Go back to your document now either by clicking anywhere in the Write window, or via the Task List.

9. Choose **Edit ➤ Paste**, or press Ctrl+V to paste the character into the document.

Figure 5.9 shows how the sample document should look now.

FIGURE 5.9:
Sample document with a special character, printed at 72 point (1-inch tall) size in the upper left corner.

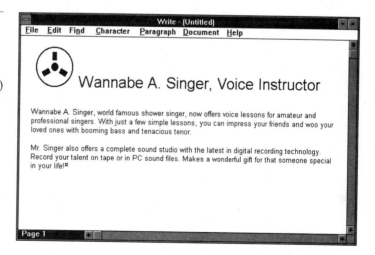

TIP *If the special character doesn't look right after copying it into your document, chances are the wrong font is selected. Select the character, then choose **Character ➤ Fonts** and the appropriate font and size. Choose OK, then click the mouse button to deselect the character.*

PRINTING A DOCUMENT

In most Windows applications, you can print the document that's currently on the screen by choosing **File ➤ Print** from the application's menu bar. Here's how you can print your current Write document now:

1. Choose **File ➤ Print** from the Write window's menu bar.
2. Choose OK.

It may take a moment for the printer to start going. If you see an error message indicating that Print Manager could not print the document, choose Cancel. See Print Manager in the Reference (or the application's help system) for more information.

SAVING A DOCUMENT

Word processor documents, like other types of files, need to be saved on disk. To save your document right now:

1. Choose **File ➤ Save**.
2. Type a file name (**singer**, if you're following the example) and choose OK.

Write will automatically add the extension .wri to the file name you provide.

EXITING WRITE

Let's leave Write now, and return to Program Manager. Follow these steps:

1. Choose **File ➤ Exit** from the Write menu bar, or double-click its Control-Menu box.

2. To close the Accessories window, double-click its Control-Menu box.

3. If you're ready to take a break, exit Windows now by choosing **File ➤ Exit Windows**. Then choose OK.

THE BIGGER PICTURE

Cutting and pasting text *within* an application is handy for general text editing. But you can use cut-and-paste to copy and move text between applications and documents as well.

CUTTING AND PASTING BETWEEN APPLICATIONS

Let's say you want to copy a name and address from an index card in Cardfile into a Write document. In Cardfile, you'd need to get to the card that contains the information, select the text on the card, and choose **Edit ➤ Copy**.

To paste the selected text into a Write document, just get to the Write document, move the insertion point to where you want to paste the text, and choose **Edit ➤ Paste**.

You can cut-and-paste text between virtually any Windows applications. You can even cut-and-paste between most DOS applications and Windows applications. As you'll see in upcoming lessons, you can also combine text and pictures using cut-and-paste, as well as Object Linking and Embedding (OLE) techniques.

ART WITH WORDS

Fonts and special characters are a great way to spruce up text in a document. But there are also tools that you can use to shape and embellish text.

Bitstream's MakeUp, shown in Figure 5.10, lets you do just about anything imaginable with text. It's easy (and fun) to use, and it supports OLE (Lesson 7), which makes it easy to import text to any document.

FIGURE 5.10:
Examples of text created with Bitstream's MakeUp.

FOR MORE INFORMATION

See the following Reference entries to learn more about topics introduced in this lesson:

Cut-And-Paste

Drives, Directories, and Files

Fonts

Special Characters

Selecting Text

Write

Working with Pictures

The ease with which today's personal computers can incorporate graphics has made the "plain vanilla" document a thing of the past. Windows applications can work with graphic images from many sources: clip art, drawings you create, scanned pictures and photos, a videotape image captured with a "frame grabber," charts from spreadsheet and graphics programs, and so forth. Figure 6.1 shows some examples.

FIGURE 6.1:

Graphic images you can use in Windows can come from a variety of sources.

**Free-hand artwork
Clip-Art**

**Bitmap images,
wallpapers**

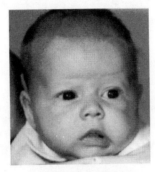

**Scanned picture, photo,
signature, or video frame**

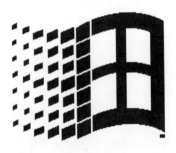

Text (special character)

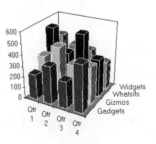

Business chart

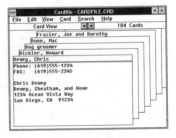

Screen capture

In this lesson, you'll get started with Paintbrush, a handy Windows tool for working with pictures. Paintbrush works with *bitmap* pictures; other applications work with other types of pictures. But many of the techniques you learn here for using Paintbrush pictures will carry over nicely to more sophisticated drawing applications you may use in the future.

STARTING PAINTBRUSH

To start Paintbrush:

1. Open the Accessories group in Program Manager.
2. Double-click the Paintbrush icon.
3. To give yourself elbow room for drawing in, maximize the Paintbrush window now.

Figure 6.2 shows how Paintbrush first appears and identifies several of its features, described below:

Drawing area: You can draw and work within the drawing area only. Any space outside it is "dead space" you can't use. Initially, the drawing area may be larger than your screen, in which case scroll bars appear along the top and bottom edges of the drawing area, and there is no empty square box on the screen.

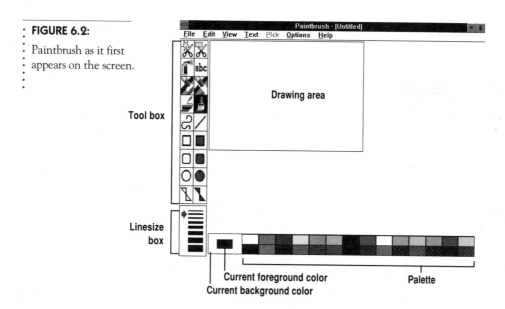

FIGURE 6.2:
Paintbrush as it first
appears on the screen.

Tool box: Tools for drawing, as well as erasing and selecting part of a drawing (See Figure 6.3). These are common tools found in many Windows graphics applications. To use a tool, click the tool you want, then drag the mouse around the drawing area.

Linesize box: When using a tool that draws lines, clicking a line width determines how wide the line will be.

Palette: Lets you choose a foreground and background color for the current tool. To choose a foreground color, click it with the left mouse button. To choose a background color, click with the right button. The current foreground and background colors appear in the Selected Color box.

FIGURE 6.3:

Tools in the tool box.

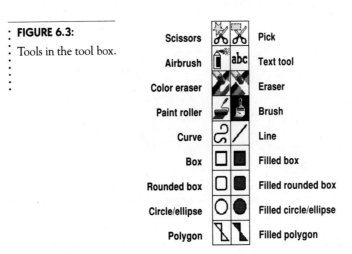

Scissors	Pick
Airbrush	Text tool
Color eraser	Eraser
Paint roller	Brush
Curve	Line
Box	Filled box
Rounded box	Filled rounded box
Circle/ellipse	Filled circle/ellipse
Polygon	Filled polygon

STARTING A PICTURE

The first step to creating a picture is to decide on a size and whether you want colors or black-and-white. Before we get started, I should mention that Paintbrush is one of the few applications that use both the left and right mouse buttons. *Left-click* in this lesson means "click the left mouse button." *Right-click* means "click the mouse button on the right."

1. To start with a clean slate and "neutral" colors, left-click black (sets the foreground to black), then right-click white (sets the background to white).

2. Choose **Options ➤ Image Attributes**. You'll see the dialog box shown in Figure 6.4.

The default, and maximum, size of your drawing area is determined by the resolution of your screen and your system memory.

3. If you know what size you want your picture to be, choose one of the Units options (e.g., **in** for inches). Then enter a width and a height (in inches). If you just want to maximize your drawing area, choose Default. (The example that follows uses this setting.)

4. Choose Colors or Black and White. (Choose Colors now if you're following along.)

5. Choose OK.

FIGURE 6.4:

The Image Attributes dialog box lets you predefine the size, and either Colors or Black and White, for a new drawing.

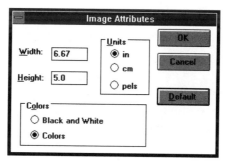

CREATING A SIMPLE LOGO

If you're as artistically inept as myself, you may need a little help with your drawing. This section shows how you can use one of the TrueType special characters as a starting point for creating a logo. If you follow these steps hands-on, you'll have a convenient "object" to use for linking and embedding in Lesson 7.

If you want to try your hand at drawing a picture from scratch, see PaintBrush in the Reference for information on the drawing tools.

1. Click the Text tool (abc), then click near the upper-left corner of the drawing area.

2. Choose **Text ➤ Fonts**.

3. Choose the Wingdings font.

4. Click the Size box, and type in **144** as the font size (about two inches).

5. Choose OK.

6. Press ↵ to move the insertion point down (so you can see the entire insertion point).

7. Use the Character Map or simply type Shift+[to insert the Wingdings flower character shown in Figure 6.5.

FIGURE 6.5:

A flower, which is actually a special character displayed at 144 point, in Paintbrush.

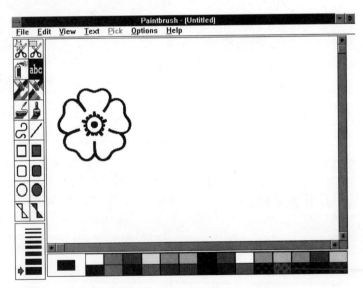

You can find any special character and its keystroke equivalent inside the back cover of this book.

If you didn't get it quite right the first time, press Backspace to erase whatever character you brought to the screen, then try again.

ADDING COLOR

To add color within an image in Paintbrush, follow these steps:

1. Choose the Paint Roller tool.
2. Select a color from the palette by left-clicking.
3. Point anywhere within an enclosed area and click.

The color you've chosen will fill the area. If the area is not fully enclosed, the color will fill the entire background area. If you want to practice color-filling now, try out different colors in the petals and center area of the flower.

SAVING THE PICTURE

To save your picture for use in later lessons:

1. Choose **File ➤ Save**.
2. Type in a file name, such as **myflower**, and then choose OK.

Paintbrush will automatically add the extension .bmp to the file name.

STARTING WITH A CLEAN SLATE

Whenever you have saved a picture and are ready to begin another, you should first clear the screen colors to start with a clean slate:

1. Left-click black, then right-click white in the palette.

2. Choose **File ➤ New**.

CAPTURING A SCREEN IMAGE

Another source of graphic images is Windows' screen-capturing ability. Just press the PrintScreen key (or Alt+Shift+PrintScreen) to copy the current screen to the Clipboard, from which you can paste it into Paintbrush (or any Windows application that supports graphics) for further work.

Figure 6.6 shows the Sound Recorder icon pasted into the Paintbrush drawing area, cropped and resized (to be embedded as a logo in Lesson 7).

Take the following steps if you want to practice this procedure:

1. Minimize Paintbrush and open the Accessories group in Program Manager. Make sure the Sound Recorder icon is visible.

2. Press PrintScreen to capture the current window to the Clipboard.

FIGURE 6.6:

An icon captured from the Program Manager screen, cropped and resized in Paintbrush.

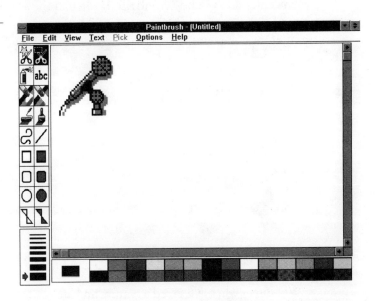

TIP

Use the Clipboard Viewer (double-click the Clipboard icon in the Main group) to verify the contents of the Clipboard at any time.

3. Reopen and (if necessary) maximize Paintbrush.

4. Choose **Edit ➤ Paste**.

It may take a little trial-and-error to get exactly the portion of the screen you want (in this case, the microphone) captured and pasted.

CROPPING AN IMAGE

Whether you've pasted a screen-capture or imported some other image into Paintbrush, you may not want to work with the whole drawing. To crop an image, drag the Pick tool (scissors-and-square) across the desired area and cut it to the Clipboard (**Edit ➤ Cut**). To get rid of the unwanted material, open a new file without saving the old one. Then paste the cropped image into the blank drawing area.

Here's how you would isolate the microphone from the Program Manager screen in our example:

1. Place the Pick tool just above and to the left of the microphone.

2. Drag the mouse diagonally until the entire microphone is selected (outlined).

3. Choose **Edit ➤ Cut**.

4. Choose **File ➤ New** and answer No when asked about saving the current image.

5. Choose **Edit ➤ Paste**.

SIZING AN IMAGE

The Pick menu's Shrink & Grow option is your tool for making an image larger or smaller. Here's how you would use it to resize the microphone icon:

1. With the image selected, choose **Pick ➤ Shrink & Grow** from the menu bar.

2. Choose **Pick** again and make sure Clear is checked. This option tells Paintbrush to clear the old image from the screen after resizing.

3. Place the mouse pointer above and to the left of the image.

4. Hold down the Shift key and drag the mouse to create a frame about 2 inches square.

> *Holding down the Shift key while dragging ensures that the new frame will have the same proportions as the original.*

5. Release the mouse button. The image expands to fill the new frame.

6. Choose **Pick ➤ Shrink & Grow** again to turn off that option.

7. Click anywhere outside the frame to remove the old frame.

PRINTING A PICTURE

You can print any PaintBrush picture using either the screen's or the printer's resolution. The second option sometimes produces the best result, because otherwise Paintbrush may need to stretch the drawing to reproduce the dimensions of the screen.

1. Choose **File ➤ Print**. You'll see the dialog box shown in Figure 6.7.

2. Check the Use Printer Resolution box and choose OK.

FIGURE 6.7:
Print dialog box for printing a picture from Paintbrush.

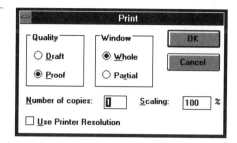

If the printed image is too small, go back to the Print dialog box and enter a higher percentage (say 300) in the Scaling text box. Experiment until you find a size you like.

To use this image in Lesson 7, save it now with a name such as **singlogo**.

OPENING AN EXISTING PICTURE

You can also use Paintbrush to open and modify any existing picture stored in bitmap format. For instance, the various wallpaper images that came with your Windows package are bitmaps. Bitmap files typically have the extensions .bmp or .dib (for device-independent bitmap). If you'd like to take a look at one of your existing bitmaps in Paintbrush now, follow these steps:

1. Choose **File ➤ New** to start with a clean drawing area.

2. Choose **File ➤ Open**. The Open file dialog box appears, and you should see several files with .bmp extensions in the list box.

3. If you plan to work through the next example, choose **winlogo.bmp**.

The bitmap image appears on your screen.

TIP

Before experimenting with an existing bitmap (or any other file that you don't want to risk changing), it's a good idea to save the current copy with a new name. That way, if you mess things up and save the new copy, your original copy will be left unharmed. Save the copy of winlogo on your screen with the name winlog2.bmp if you're following the hands-on examples.

THE DRAWING AREA AND WHITE SPACE

Unlike the images you created yourself earlier in this chapter, most existing bitmaps will be sized in such a way that they fill the entire drawing area. The white space outside the drawing area is just "dead space" that you cannot use. You can see this for yourself by using the Pick tool to frame a section of winlogo and dragging it around the screen. You'll see that you can't move the cutout outside the drawing area.

Why reduce the drawing area around a picture instead of leaving some extra white space to work with? If the picture doesn't fill the entire drawing area, all that extra white space shows up in situations where you might not want it:

- When you use Object Linking and Embedding (Lesson 7) to display the picture in a written document, the extra white space will show up, making it impossible to align the text in the document close to the picture.

- If you print the graphic at a large size (say 400% or greater), the extra white space will be printed as blank sheets of paper.

- Paintbrush stores the entire drawing area when you save the file, not just the portion you drew in. Therefore, that extra white space around your picture actually takes up disk space.

- If you were to use a picture that you created yourself as wallpaper, the white space will show up on the screen, even if you tile the wallpaper.

The simplest way to control the white space is to define the size of the drawing area *before* you start to draw, using the **Options ➤ Image Attributes** options as soon as you start Paintbrush.

RESIZING A DRAWING AREA

Although it's a little more cumbersome, you can also resize the drawing area after creating the drawing. The basic steps are these:

- Cut the portion of the picture that you want to save to the Clipboard.
- Resize the drawing area to whatever dimensions you want.
- Paste the picture back into the resized drawing area.

If you want to try this out, use the microphone logo (currently a small image in a larger drawing area). After opening singlogo.bmp, you would take the following steps:

1. To help figure out a realistic size for the drawing area, first choose **View ➤ Cursor Position**. This displays the current cursor position (in pixels) near the upper-right corner of the Paintbrush window.

> A pixel, also known as a pel, is one tiny little "dot of light" on your screen. 100 pixels equals about 1 inch.

2. Choose the Pick tool and drag a frame around the microphone that's approximately the size you want the final picture to be.

3. Once the area is framed, move (don't drag) the crosshairs to the lower-right corner of the framed area.

4. Look to the cursor position box to determine where the crosshairs are. Jot down the width and height numbers; you'll need them in a moment.

5. Now choose **Edit ➤ Cut** to cut the framed area to the Clipboard.

Now you need to create a new drawing area with the dimensions you just determined:

1. Choose **Options ➤ Image Attributes**.

2. In the Units box, choose pels.

3. Enter your new width and height settings.

4. Choose OK.

5. With the drawing safely in the Clipboard, you can ignore the warning that now appears and choose Yes to proceed.

6. Choose No when prompted to save the current drawing.

7. Choose **Edit ➤ Paste** to paste the drawing into the new, correctly sized drawing area.

8. Click the Pick tool in the toolbox to deselect the pasted image.

9. Now save the file under its old name, replacing the old file.

The first version of singlogo that you saved probably ate up around 150,000 bytes of disk space. This version probably takes up about 9,000 bytes.

Figure 6.8 shows how the image looks now. The picture fits nicely within the drawing area, which will help to simplify our linking and embedding exercises in the next lesson.

FIGURE 6.8:

Singlogo is now stored within a smaller drawing area, as indicated by the frame surrounding the picture.

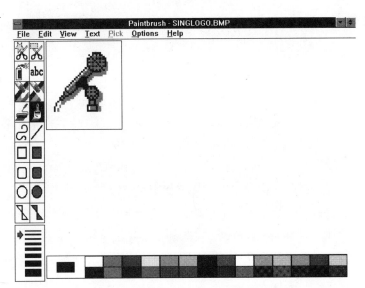

EXITING PAINTBRUSH

To exit Paintbrush and return to Program Manager, use the usual techniques for closing an application:

◆ Double-click the Control-Menu box in the upper left corner of the Paintbrush window (or choose **File ➤ Exit** from its menu bar).

If you want to take a break, you can exit Windows now.

THE BIGGER PICTURE

Graphic images come in a huge variety of formats, including .BMP (Windows bitmap), .DIB (Device Independent Bitmap), .RLE (run-length encoded), .CGM (Computer Graphics Metafile), .EPS (Encapsulated PostScript), .GIF (CompuServe Graphics Interchange Format), .PCX (PC Paintbrush), .TIF (Tagged Image File), .WMF (Windows MetaFile), and .WPG (WordPerfect Graphic), just to name a few.

One of the most amazing things about Windows 3.1 is that, nine times out of ten, you needn't worry about a particular picture's format. Using the Clipboard, you can cut-and-paste a picture from one application to another. Figure 6.9 shows a few examples where cut-and-paste was used to paste pictures into Excel, WordPerfect, and Word without any file conversion whatsoever.

For situations where you *do* need to convert files, you can use one of the shareware graphics conversion programs or a commercial program like Hijaak for Windows, from Inset Systems, which isn't free, but can convert a wide variety of graphic image file formats.

FOR MORE INFORMATION

For more information on working with pictures, and cutting-and-pasting, see these entries in the Reference:

Cut-And-Paste

Clipboard

Paintbrush

Print Screen

FIGURE 6.9:

In many situations, cut-and-paste (and OLE) will let you copy a picture from one application to the next, without converting the format of the file.

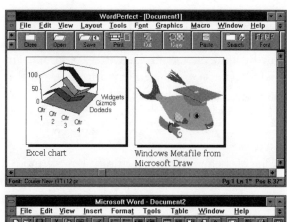

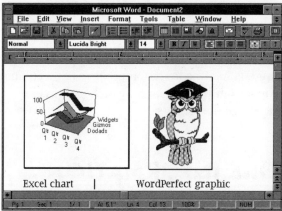

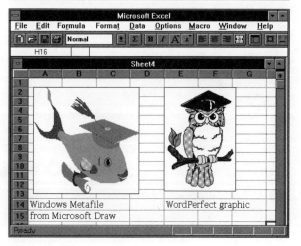

*P*ULLING IT ALL TOGETHER WITH OLE

Cut-and-Paste is one way to combine text and pictures from separate applications into a single document. But it's useful mainly with data that isn't likely to change. For instance, suppose you cut-and-paste a spreadsheet chart into several documents. If you later change the spreadsheet and its associated chart, you'd need to go back to those several other documents, and cut-and-paste the new graph again into each one—a laborious and time-consuming process.

In this lesson, you'll learn a way of combining text and pictures from multiple applications that makes updating automatic.

OLE—A BETTER WAY TO "CUT-AND-PASTE"

Object Linking and Embedding, abbreviated OLE (and pronounced oh-lay), is an alternative means of combining information from two or more applications that maintains a link between the "pasted" object and the application that was used to create it. This link makes it much easier to edit the pasted objects, as you'll see in a moment.

OLE TERMINOLOGY

Before you start using OLE, you need to understand some of the buzzwords that go along with it, as well as some restrictions on its use.

- An *object* is any single unit of information, such as a graphic image, a business chart, or a spreadsheet cell, that you've saved as a file for embedding.

- The *source document* is the document from which the object originates. For instance, if the object is part of a picture you created in Paintbrush, the entire Paintbrush picture is the source document.

- The *source application* is the application that was used to create the object, or is used to edit the object, i.e., Paintbrush in the above example.

- The destination document is the document that contains the embedded object. For instance, if you're displaying the picture in a Write document, that Write document is the destination document.

- Applications that let you create objects that can be embedded or linked into other objects are called *servers*, because they can "serve up" an object to another application.

- Applications that can accept an object are called *clients*.

Figure 7.1 illustrates this terminology with an example. There, Microsoft Excel was used to create a spreadsheet and chart. A copy of the chart appears in a Write document.

FIGURE 7.1:

Microsoft Excel was the application used to create an object (a chart), and a Windows Write document contains a copy of that object.

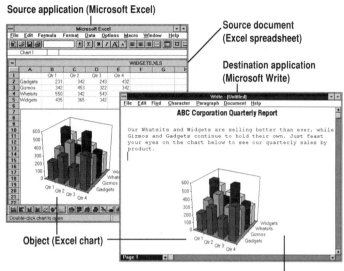

SERVERS AND CLIENTS

Only some Windows applications support OLE; and some support it only as a server, or only as a client, while some can support it as both.

Table 7.1 lists various Windows applets, and whether they act as server or client. Simply stated, a Write document or index card can contain an object you created with Paintbrush or Sound Recorder, but not vice versa.

TABLE 7.1: OLE Capabilities of Windows Applets

WINDOWS APPLET	CLIENT/SERVER
Write	Client
Cardfile	Client
Paintbrush	Server
Sound Recorder	Server

To find out whether an application not listed in Table 7.1 supports OLE (as client, server, or both), you'll need to check that application's documentation.

LINKING AND EMBEDDING

It's essential to keep in mind the difference between embedding and linking:

- When you *embed* an object, you maintain a link to the source application, but not to the original source object. Thus, when you edit the copy that's in the destination document, you're editing only that copy—not the original object. Likewise, editing the original object has no effect on the copy in the destination document.

- When you *link* an object to a destination document, you maintain a link to both the source application and the original source object. The destination document contains a "pointer" to the original object. Thus, both the source and destination documents reflect any changes you make to the original object.

SO WHEN DO I USE WHICH?

In a nutshell, you use object embedding when you plan to tailor copies of an object to the document it happens to be in at the moment; and you use object linking when you want to ensure that all client documents reflect an exact, up-to-the-minute copy of the original object.

For instance, let's say you create a spreadsheet chart that changes from time to time to reflect the current status of some data. If you want to put a copy of that chart in a document that describes data *as of* a certain date, you probably don't want that chart to change within the document. Thus, you'd use object embedding to keep the chart in the document independent of the original spreadsheet chart, which changes with time.

TIP

If you're planning to distribute copies of a document on floppy disk, you'll probably want to use object embedding, since the recipient's computer might not contain a copy of the original object to which object linking "points."

But if the document describes the chart as showing *current* data, such as "the current quarterly sales projections," using object linking would ensure that the memo did indeed display the chart with the most current data.

When would you need to use "regular" cut-and-paste? As noted earlier, some applications don't support OLE. Or you might be distributing copies on disk of a document such as our sales-projection example and don't want recipients to be able to make changes to the underlying spreadsheet data. Even if the data isn't particularly sensitive, your recipients may not have a copy of the source application used to create the object.

How to Link and Embed

There are many possible methods you can use to embed and link objects, and we won't go through every one here. But the basic technique is pretty much the same as it is for regular cut-and-paste:

- Create or open the object you want to embed or link.
- If the object is new (or "Untitled"), be sure to choose **File ➤ Save** to give it a file name. (If you don't do this, you'll end up with a regular cut-and-paste operation.)
- Select the object, or portion of the object, you want to link or embed.
- Choose **File ➤ Copy** to copy the selected object to the Clipboard.
- Open the destination document and place the insertion point where you want the object to appear.
- To embed the object, choose **Edit ➤ Paste**. To link the object, choose **Edit ➤ Paste Link**.

The following examples demonstrate embedding and linking in detail, using Paintbrush as our OLE server, and Write as our OLE client. If you're following along hands-on, you'll need the singlogo.bmp, myflower.bmp, and singer.wri files from earlier lessons.

EMBEDDING AN OBJECT

This procedure uses the singlogo and singer files to demonstrate the steps for embedding an object.

COPYING THE OBJECT TO THE CLIPBOARD

You first need to get the source object (in this case, the logo) you created back onto the screen. Follow these steps:

1. Open the source application (in this example, Paintbrush) and maximize its window.

2. Use **File ➤ Open** to open the file containing the object you want (in this example, singlogo.bmp).

3. If necessary (as it is here), select the portion of the file to embed. (Here, you would use the Pick tool to drag a frame around the microphone, as in Figure 7.2.)

4. Choose **Edit ➤ Copy** to copy the selection to the Clipboard.

5. Close the source application.

EMBEDDING THE OBJECT INTO THE DOCUMENT

Once the Clipboard contains a copy of the object, you can easily embed it into the destination document. Follow these steps:

1. Open the destination document. (In this case, start Write and choose the singer.wri file.) For a little elbow room, you may want to maximize the document window.

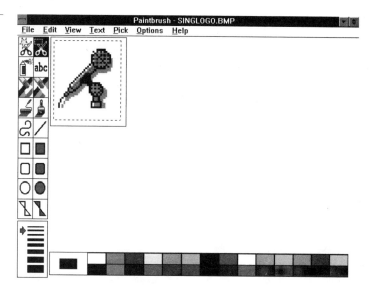

FIGURE 7.2:

Area to be copied to
the Clipboard is
framed.

2. Place the insertion point where you want to display the object (in this example, press Ctrl+Home to move to the top of the document).

3. Choose **Edit ➤ Paste** to paste in the object (in this case, the new logo).

4. To save this new copy of the document, choose **File ➤ Save**.

5. To print the new copy of the document, choose **File ➤ Print**, then choose OK.

If you're following along on-line, your screen should resemble Figure 7.3.

Unlike Write, most of the more advanced word processors, such as Word for Windows and WordPerfect for Windows, will let you wrap text around a picture that you've pasted into a document.

The difference between embedding and the standard cut-and-paste techniques isn't yet apparent. Behind the scenes, however, you've established a link between the Write document and Paintbrush; this link will make editing the embedded object much easier.

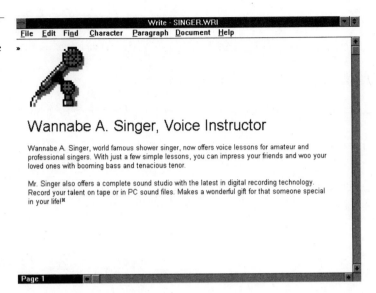

FIGURE 7.3:

The singlogo picture is embedded in the Write document.

EDITING AN EMBEDDED OBJECT

When you've embedded an object, you can edit it easily without leaving the destination document:

- Double-click anywhere in the embedded object (here, the microphone logo).

Figure 7.4 shows the result: Windows instantly restarts the source application (Paintbrush) and displays the object (the microphone) ready for editing.
Notice that the title bar shows:

Paintbrush: Paintbrush Picture in SINGER.WRI

You are not editing your original logo. Rather, you're editing only the copy within your Write document. If you're following along on-line, you can see this for yourself:

1. In Paintbrush, add a background color or make some other minor change to the image.

2. From the Paintbrush menu bar, choose **File**. Notice the last option in the File menu: **Exit & return to SINGER.WRI**. Windows "knows" that you got here from a Write document. Choose this option now.

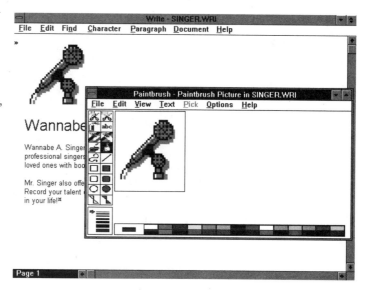

3. You'll see the message shown in Figure 7.5. In plain English, it's asking whether to carry the changes you just made to the Write document. Choose Yes.

4. Click anywhere below the logo to deselect it.

Now you're back to your Write document, and can see the changes you made to the logo within your document. Remember that your changes have affected only this copy of the logo. Your initial singlogo.bmp logo still has its original white background.

Nonetheless, the fact that you embedded the logo in the Write document gave you a quick shortcut back to Paintbrush. All you had to do was double-click the logo to get instant access to Paintbrush.

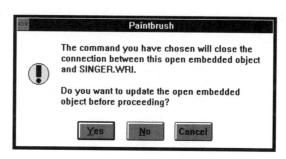

You could go back to Paintbrush and reload your original copy of singlogo.bmp to verify that it has not been changed. You don't need to do that right now, however, because we'll be paste-linking that object into the document in a moment. There, you'll see the original, unchanged logo.

Before we can link a copy of that object into the current document, you need to delete the embedded copy. Just click that copy now, to select it, and press Delete.

LINKING AN OBJECT

The procedure for linking differs from embedding only in the last step:

- With the object in the Clipboard and the insertion point positioned in the document, choose **Edit ➤ Paste Link**, rather than Paste.

(If you've been working through this example, a copy of the original microphone logo is still in the Clipboard. So you need only choose **Edit ➤ Paste Link** now to link it.)

Here, again, the differences from other paste operations aren't apparent yet; but watch what happens when you edit the linked object.

EDITING THE LINKED OBJECT

To begin editing a linked object from its destination document, double-click it. The logo is, once again, instantly loaded into Paintbrush. But notice that this time, the title bar says we are editing singlogo.bmp, the original logo, not just the copy in the Write document. Now let's see what happens when you edit the original copy:

1. Once again, make some minor change and choose **File ➤ Exit**.

2. This time, there is no message about "Closing the link..." because you have edited your original singlogo.bmp picture. Choose Yes now to save the changes you just made to the original logo, and return to Write.

3. Click any text below the logo to deselect it and see how it really looks.

Your changes to the original picture are reflected in the copy in Write. To fully appreciate what linking offers, suppose you link the logo to a dozen different documents, rather than just one. If you then change singlogo.bmp in any one of those documents, that change will be reflected in all 12 of them automatically. That saves you from having to open and change all 12 documents.

The only difference you'd notice is that, whenever you open a document that contains links to other document, Windows will ask if you want to update the links to other documents, by presenting a message like the one shown in Figure 7.6.

When you see such a message, all you need to do is choose Yes to keep all the links among the various documents up to date.

FIGURE 7.6:

Message that appears when you open a document that contains links to other documents.

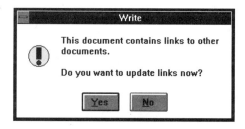

> This document contains links to other documents.
>
> Do you want to update links now?
>
> Yes   No

If you choose No in response to the question shown in Figure 7.6, any changes you made to the original document won't be reflected in the copy of the document you're opening. But you can then choose **Edit ➤ Links**, *and then choose Update Now to update the link. See Object Linking and Embedding in the Reference for more information.*

A QUICK SUMMARY OF LINKING AND EMBEDDING

As you've seen here, the procedures for cutting-and-pasting, embedding, and linking are nearly identical. The differences lie in your options after the fact. To help you keep it all straight when working on your own, Table 7.2 summarizes the different effects of these three techniques.

OBJECT PACKAGER

Another way to embed or link an object to a document is through Object Packager. With this standard accessory, the destination document contains only a "package," in the form of an icon, representing the embedded object. Opening the package (by double-clicking it) displays the linked object. You can package applications and

TABLE 7.2: Comparison of Cut-and-Paste, Object Embedding, and Object Linking

CAPABILITIES	CUT-AND-PASTE	OBJECT EMBEDDING	OBJECT LINKING
Double-click object returns to source application?	No	Yes	Yes
Double-click edits what object?	None	Copy in current document only	Original object and current copy
Changes made to original object through source application reflected in destination document(s)?	No	No	Yes
Commands used when pasting	**Edit ➤ Paste** (saved or unsaved object)	**Edit ➤ Paste** (object must have a file name)	**Edit ➤ Paste Link** (object must have a file name)
Works with...	Any application	Applications that support OLE	Applications that support OLE

run them, or package sounds and play them. For example, a multimedia demonstration might include a "sampler" of sound files the user could try out by selecting different icons.

There are two basic steps to using Object Packager:

- Create the package, and copy it to the Clipboard.
- Paste the package from the Clipboard to the destination document.

If you have a sound card, a snippet of speech or music would be an ideal candidate for trying out the following procedure. If you don't, you can use the myflower.bmp drawing (but then you'll see that for drawings, packaging offers no particular advantage over linking or embedding).

CREATING THE PACKAGE

To begin creating a package, start with the Accessories group open.

1. Double-click the Object Packager icon in the Accessories group. You'll see the dialog box shown in Figure 7.7.

2. First you need to pick an icon for the package, so click the Insert Icon button. You'll see the Insert Icon dialog box, as shown in Figure 7.8.

3. Scroll through the available icons and choose one by clicking OK. (Optionally, if you don't find an icon you like in the progman.exe set, try the other set by typing **moricons.dll** in the File Name text box, and pressing ↵. We used this set to select the multimedia icon you'll see in Figure 7.9.) A copy of the icon appears in the Appearance part of the dialog box.

FIGURE 7.7:

The Object Packager dialog box

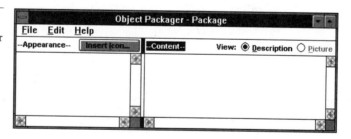

FIGURE 7.8:

The Insert Icon dialog box lets you choose an icon for your package.

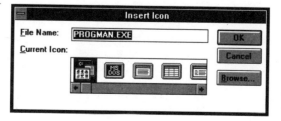

4. Now click anywhere in the Content side of the dialog box (or press Tab) and choose **File ➤ Import** from the Object Packager menu bar.

5. Choose the file you want to package (in our example, myflower.bmp).

Your dialog box should now look something like Figure 7.9. Now you need to paste this package into a document.

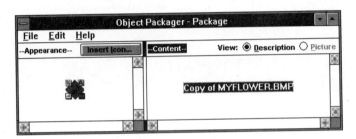

FIGURE 7.9:

The icon on the left now contains a copy of the file indicated on the right side of the dialog box.

COPYING THE PACKAGE TO A DOCUMENT

To copy the package to a document:

1. Choose **Edit ➤ Copy Package** from the Object Packager menu. A copy of the package is now placed in the Clipboard.

2. Exit Object Packager by double-clicking its Control-menu box or choosing **File ➤ Exit** from its menu bar.

3. Open the destination document (singer.wri, in our example) and position the insertion point.

4. Choose **Edit ➤ Paste** or **➤ Paste Link.** A copy of the package appears in the document, as shown in Figure 7.10.

TIP

You can also embed a package in a document simply by dragging the object's file name from File Manager into the document. See Lesson 8 and Object Linking and Embedding in the Reference.

FIGURE 7.10:

A package, and instructions for using it, in the Singer document.

ADDING INSTRUCTIONS

Figure 7.10 also shows a line of instructions for using the packaged object: *Double-click the icon to see a beautiful flower!* Because object packaging is particularly useful for documents that will be used interactively, you may often want to include such a prompt in the destination document. Glance ahead to Figure 8.7 for another example of a document that includes instructions for opening a package.

- To make the instructions conspicuous, set a new font and size. (In the example, we chose Arial 14-point from Write's **Character ➤ Fonts** dialog box.)

- Type your instructions.

Now you can give it a test run by double-clicking the icon to open the package. Exit the application whenever you're ready to return to the original document.

If you're ready to take a break, save your work and exit Windows now.

THE BIGGER PICTURE

Cut-and-paste and OLE let you take advantage of your applications' various capabilities by combining information from a variety of applications into a single document. For instance, Figure 7.11 shows a sample compound document (a document containing text and pictures from several different applications) created in WordPerfect for Windows. The ABC Corporation logo was created in Bitstream's Makeup, and the spreadsheet table and chart are from Microsoft's Excel.

FIGURE 7.11:

Sample WordPerfect for Windows document containing a logo created in Bitstream's Makeup, and a spreadsheet table and chart from Microsoft Excel.

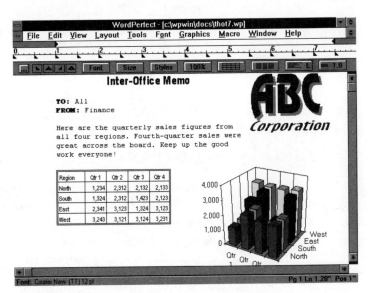

FOR MORE INFORMATION

For more information on the topics introduced in this lesson, see the following Reference entries:

Cut-And-Paste

Object Linking and Embedding

Object Packager

Sound

USING FILE
MANAGER AND
PRINT MANAGER

This lesson kills two birds with one stone. It introduces two of Windows' most important applications, File Manager and Print Manager, and it gives hands-on practice using *drag-and-drop*, a natural and pleasant way to perform many common tasks in Windows.

STARTING FILE MANAGER

File Manager is a handy tool for performing "general housekeeping" on your computer. You can use it to search for files, move, copy, and rename files, run applications, create directories and subdirectories, and more. This lesson shows how to view and select drives, directories, and files for File Manager operations, and it demonstrates the drag-and-drop technique for copying files between drives. For other operations, see File Manager in the Reference.

To start File Manager:

1. Open the Main group and double-click the File Manager icon.

2. If you want more room to work in, maximize or resize File Manager.

File Manager appears on the desktop, as shown in Figure 8.1. The *directory window* that appears presents a graphical overview of the drives on your system, the directories on the current drive, and the files on the current directory.

> *If your directory window displays only the directory tree, or only file names, choose* **View** ➤ **Tree and Directory***.*

File Manager offers a perfect tool to "go exploring," since you can see at a glance what drives and directories are available, and what files are stored on each directory.

FIGURE 8.1:

File Manager showing directories on drive c, and files on c:\windows.

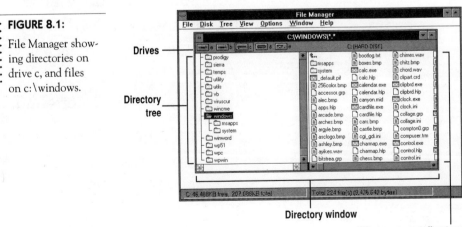

CHOOSING A DRIVE

You can switch to another drive simply by clicking the drive's button. When you choose a new drive, the directory tree changes to reflect the directory names (if any) on that drive.

WARNING

If you choose an empty floppy drive (A or B) or CD-ROM drive, you'll see an error message indicating that the drive is empty. Either insert a formatted disk and choose Retry, or choose Cancel to stay on the current drive.

CHOOSING A DIRECTORY

The directory tree shows the directories on the current drive. Each directory contains its own set of files, some of them grouped into additional subdirectories.

TIP

The highest level directory on a drive is called the root *directory. Technically, all directories beneath the root are subdirectories. But it's common practice to call them all directories.*

If there are more directories on the current drive than can fit into the window, the scroll bars are activated, so you can scroll through the tree. The name of the current directory is highlighted in the directory tree, and its file folder icon is open. The file names to the right of the directory tree are the files on the current directory (or subdirectory) only.

To view the files on another directory, simply click the name of the directory you want to switch to. The list of file names instantly changes to show the names of files on the selected directory.

To expand a directory, to see if it contains any subdirectories ("branches"), double-click the directory name. To collapse the directory (hide its subdirectory names), double-click the directory name a second time.

VIEWING SUBDIRECTORIES

If you're not sure whether a particular directory contains subdirectories, just choose **Tree ➤ Indicate Expandable Branches**. Directories with expandable branches will be indicated by a plus sign in the directory icon. When all the subdirectories are displayed, this changes to a minus sign.

You can also use any of the following techniques to expand or collapse the directory tree to view more, or fewer subdirectories:

- Choose **Tree ➤ Expand One Level**, or press + to expand the current directory by one level.

- Choose **Tree ➤ Expand Branch**, or press * to expand the current directory to its fullest.

- Choose **Tree ➤ Expand All**, or press Ctrl+* (using the gray * key on the numeric keypad) to expand the entire directory tree to its fullest.

- Choose **Tree ➤ Collapse Branch** to collapse the current directory so that none of its subdirectories appears anymore.

- To widen the directory tree portion of the display, choose **View ➤ Split**, move the mouse to the right to indicate how wide you want the directory tree display to be, then click the mouse button. (Optionally, you can just drag the Split Bar, without choosing the menu options first.)

- To display only the first level of directories, first double-click the root directory (\ ) at the top of the tree to collapse the entire tree. Then double-click that same icon again to expand the tree one level.

VIEWING FILE NAMES

If there are more file names on the current directory than can fit within the window, scroll bars appear at the bottom and/or right edge of the file names. You can use the scroll bars to scroll through file names.

Icons in the Files area of the directory window indicate the type of information each file contains, as summarized in Table 8.1.

TABLE 8.1: File Manager Icons

ICON	MEANING
	Up a Level: Click this icon to move up a level in the directory tree.
	Subdirectories: Always listed before file names. Click any subdirectory name to move down to that subdirectory.
	Application Files: Double-clicking an application icon starts that application. Exiting the application returns you to File Manager.
	Document Files: Documents associated with a given application. Double-clicking one of these icons starts the application with the document file already loaded. Exiting the application returns you to File Manager.
	System or Hidden Files: Files that are hidden or are used only by the computer. Never move or delete one of these unless you are sure you know what you are doing.
	All other files: Most commonly used to identify files that are not associated with a particular application.

You can also choose how you want to view file names:

◆ Choose **View ➤ Name** to view only file names.

◆ Choose **View ➤ Partial Details**, choose what details you want to see by clicking the check box next to each, then choose OK.

◆ Choose **View ➤ All File Details** to view the name of each file, its size, the date and time of its most recent change, and its attributes. (You may need to widen the directory tree window to see all of this information.)

SELECTING FILES FOR A TASK

In some situations, you might want to use File Manager to copy or move several files from one directory to another (or to a floppy disk). There are several ways to select files to work with:

◆ To select a file for some operation, click (once) on the file name. (Any previously selected file names are instantly deselected.)

◆ To select a second file, hold down the Ctrl key and click the name of the file.

◆ To extend the current selection to include several files, hold down Shift and Ctrl, and click the last file name in the group you want to select.

◆ To deselect a single file, hold down the Ctrl key and click the name of the selected file.

◆ To deselect all the currently selected files, just click any one file without holding down a key (only that file will be selected now.)

As you select files, the indicator near the bottom of the File Manager window shows how many files are selected, and how many bytes they contain, as Figure 8.2 shows.

TIP

When copying files to a floppy disk, use the "bytes" indicator to avoid choosing more files than will fit on the floppy disk.

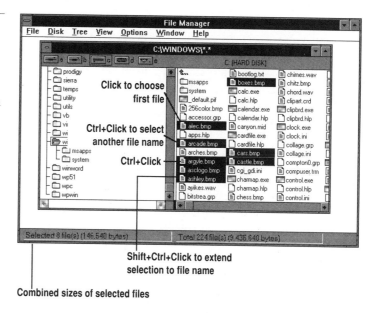

FIGURE 8.2:

Numerous files selected in File Manager. The indicator at the bottom of the screen shows how many bytes the selected files contain.

Click to choose first file

Ctrl+Click to select another file name

Ctrl+Click

Shift+Ctrl+Click to extend selection to file name

Combined sizes of selected files

VIEWING MULTIPLE DIRECTORIES

You can open any number of directory windows, to see the contents of more than one directory at a time. Viewing multiple directories is also handy for copying and moving files and directories. To open a second directory window:

1. Choose **Window ➤ New Window**.

2. In the new directory window, choose the drive and/or directory that you want to view.

3. Optionally, you can size and move the directory tree windows, with the usual sizing and moving techniques (or by choosing **Window ➤ Tile**) to get a better view of each directory.

USING DRAG-AND-DROP TO COPY FILES

Perhaps the best way to get a feel for using File Manager would be to copy some files to a floppy disk. If you've been following along, you've created (among others),

121

singer.wri (a Write document), and singlogo.bmp (a Paintbrush picture), and you can use those files in the steps that follow:

1. Place a blank, formatted floppy disk in drive A or drive B of your computer, and close the drive door.

2. If you haven't already done so, open a second directory window by choosing **Window ➤ New Window**.

3. In the second directory window, click the appropriate floppy drive button.

4. Now size and move the windows so that you can see at least some portion of each window, as in Figure 8.3.

5. Click the title bar of the Windows directory window (not the A or B drive directory window), to make it active.

6. For convenience, choose **View ➤ Name** to view only file names, then choose **View ➤ Sort by Name** to put the names into alphabetical order.

7. Choose two or more files (singer.wri and singlogo.bmp in this example) by clicking once on the first file, holding down the Ctrl key, and clicking (once) on the second file. Both file names should now be selected, as in Figure 8.4.

FIGURE 8.3:

Two directory windows open in File Manager; one for the Windows directory on the hard disk, one for the floppy disk in drive A.

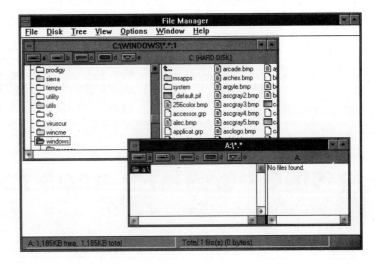

: Two file names,
: singer.wri and
: singlogo.bmp, are
: selected.

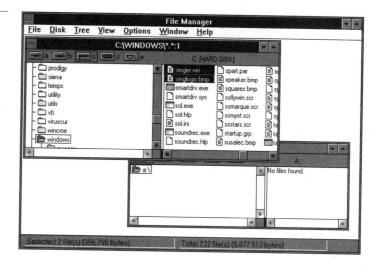

If you made a mistake, and selected too many, or too few file names, just repeat Step 7.

COPYING THE SELECTED FILES

Once you've selected the files you want to copy, you can copy them simply by dragging their icons with your mouse. Follow these steps:

1. Move the mouse pointer to any of the selected files, *hold down* (don't click) the mouse button, and drag the icon to the files area of the directory window for drive A (or to the A drive button, or the A:\ file icon). Then release the mouse button.

2. When you see the prompt asking if you're sure you want to copy the files, choose Yes.

TIP *Always read the message that appears after you release the mouse button to see if the file will be moved, or copied. If File Manager intends to move the files, and you meant to copy them, choose No.*

3. When the Copying... window disappears, you can click anywhere in the directory window for drive A to verify that it now contains copies of the files, as illustrated in Figure 8.5.

4. Before removing the floppy (and labeling it), close the directory window (double-click its Control-Menu bar).

· **FIGURE 8.5:**
·
· Two files copied to
· the disk in drive A.

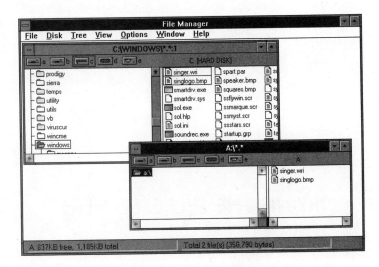

If you don't first close the directory window before you remove a floppy from its drive, File Manager will attempt to view an empty drive. Also, if you change the floppy in drive A or B while the directory window is still open, the directory window won't automatically reflect the change. You'll need to refresh the window by clicking the drive button again, or by choosing **Window ➤ Refresh***.*

DRAG-AND-DROP ASSUMPTIONS

If you aren't paying close attention to the screen while dragging directories and file names, you may inadvertently move a file you intended to copy. To avoid mistakes, keep in mind the following assumptions:

- If you drag a file name to a different drive, File Manager assumes you want to *copy* the file. (The icon you're dragging will contain a plus sign.)

- If you drag the file name to a different directory on the same drive, File Manager assumes you want to *move* the file. (The icon you're dragging will *not* contain a plus sign.)

WARNING

Moving directories and application files can have negative consequences, because File Manager does not automatically update system files, such as config.sys, autoexec.bat, win.ini, and system.ini after the move. Unless you know how to edit those system files, stick to copying files, or limit your moves to document files only.

You can override File Manager's assumptions by using the Ctrl and Alt keys:

- To ensure that the file will be copied, rather than moved, hold down the Ctrl key while keeping the mouse button depressed. The Move icon changes to a Copy icon. Release the mouse button before you release the Ctrl key.

- To ensure that the file will be moved, rather than copied, hold down the Alt key while keeping the mouse button depressed. The Copy icon changes to a Move icon. Release the mouse button before you release the Alt key.

TIP

To remember which key does which in drag-and-drop, just remember that both Ctrl and Copy begin with the letter C.

DRAG-AND-DROP PRINTING

Print Manager does most of its work behind the scenes, handling all printing in Windows applications. We rarely need to work with it directly, because we can just choose **File ➤ Print** from an application's menu bar. When you want to print several files from different applications in succession, however, Print Manager (together with File Manager and the drag-and-drop technique) provides a convenient shortcut. Just drag whatever document file you want to print to the Print Manager icon.

Here's the procedure in detail; you can use singer.wri if you want to try it now.

SETTING UP THE DESKTOP FOR DRAG-AND-DROP PRINTING

The first stage is to arrange the desktop so that file icons can be dragged from File Manager onto the Print Manager icon for printing:

1. If necessary, open and minimize the File Manager window.

2. In the Main group, double-click the Print Manager icon to open Print Manager. It appears as in Figure 8.6.

3. If you've installed several printers, choose one to use for printing right now.

4. Minimize Print Manager and reopen File Manager.

5. If File Manager is currently maximized, click its Restore button.

6. As necessary, size and move the window so that you can see the Print Manager's icon on the desktop.

FIGURE 8.6:

Print Manager, as it first appears on the screen.

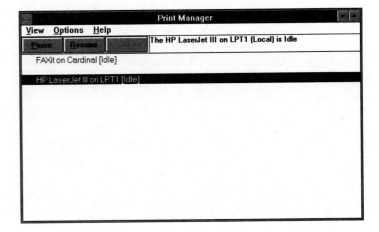

PRINTING THE FILE

With File Manager and Print Manager arranged in this fashion, you can now print any document file by dragging its icon to the Print Manager icon. Follow these steps to try it out:

1. If necessary, choose the drive and directory to get to your Windows directory.

2. Select the file (in this case, singer.wri).

3. Drag the file's icon onto the Print Manager icon and release the mouse button.

4. If, as in this example, the document contains links to other documents, Windows will ask if you want to update the links before printing. Choose Yes.

5. The Print dialog box for Write appears. Choose OK to print the document.

Your document will start printing in a moment. When the job is done, you'll be returned to File Manager. To print more documents, continue dragging their icons to the Print Manager. Using this method, you won't need to open each document's application.

If you're working through the examples, close File Manager and Print Manager now.

LIMITATIONS AND SHORTCUTS

There are a few limitations, and shortcuts, to keep in mind when using the drag-and-drop method to print files:

- You can select only one document file to print before dragging it to Print Manager's icon. If multiple files are selected, you'll see an error message.

- You can print *only* document files that are associated with some application. (For information on associating files with applications, see File Manager in the Reference.)

◆ As an alternative to dragging-and-dropping, you can simply select the document file you want to print, then choose **File ➤ Print** from File Manager's menu bar.

◆ For more information on how you can use Print Manager to solve printing problems, install a new printer, and so forth, see Print Manager in the Reference.

THE BIGGER PICTURE

Here are some more drag-and-drop techniques you can try out on your own.

USING DRAG-AND-DROP TO EMBED A PACKAGE

You can use drag-and-drop as a quick-and-easy alternative to Object Packager to place a package in a document.

Open the target document, then open File Manager. Size and position the windows so you can see both applications. Drag the document or application file from File Manager into the document at the place where you want the package to appear. When you release the mouse button, a default icon for the package appears, followed by the name of the file (see Figure 8.7). Double-clicking that icon will then open the package.

USING DRAG-AND-DROP TO MOVE AND COPY TEXT

Some Windows word processors and spreadsheets also let you move text in a document by dropping and dragging. The common technique is similar to the drag-and-drop operations you've just tried out:

◆ Select the text you want to move, including any surrounding spaces that may be needed in its new location.

◆ To move the text, just hold down the mouse button. To copy the text, first press (and hold down) the Ctrl key, then hold down the mouse button. The mouse pointer changes to an icon showing that a move or copy operation is in progress (Figure 8.8).

FIGURE 8.7:

You can drag-and-drop a file name into any document that supports OLE to create an instant package.

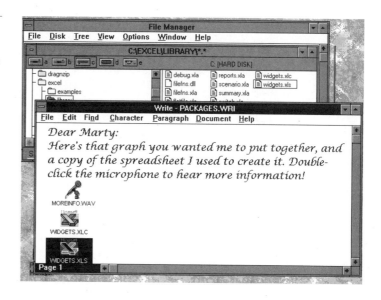

FIGURE 8.8:

Text to be moved or copied is selected in Word for Windows (version 2.0).

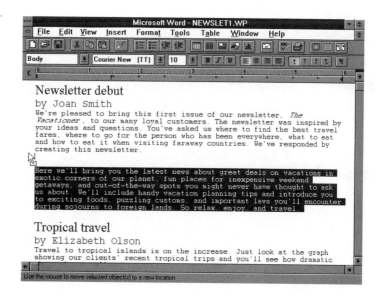

♦ Drag the mouse pointer to wherever you want to move (or copy) the text.

♦ Release the mouse button (then the Ctrl key if you're copying) to move or copy the text to the current mouse pointer position.

To learn more about drag-and-drop in your particular word processing (or other) application, see that application's documentation.

USING DRAG-AND-DROP TO MANAGE ICONS

You can also use drag-and-drop to move and copy icons from one group to another. You'll see an example in the next lesson, where you'll copy a couple of icons from the Accessories group window to the Startup group window.

FOR MORE INFORMATION

For more information on the applications and techniques introduced in this lesson, see:

Drives, Directories, and Files

Icons

File Manager

Print Manager

Program Manager

STREAMLINING WINDOWS

In this lesson we'll look at some handy tips and shortcuts for running applications and loading documents into applications, as well as other techniques for streamlining your day-to-day use of Windows. We'll start with a simple but useful trick for automatically loading frequently used document files.

AUTOLOADING DOCUMENT FILES

Although you'll usually want to start an application with an empty document on the screen, it may sometimes make sense to have an application start with a particular document file already loaded. For example, you might want to start Cardfile with your index cards, and Calendar with your appointments, already loaded.

To have an application start with a document already loaded, you change the application's properties. In the Program Item Properties dialog box, follow the application's startup command with a space and the name of the document you want to load. We can demonstrate the procedure using Cardfile as an example.

AUTOLOADING YOUR PERSONAL INDEX CARDS

To autoload your personal index cards every time you start Cardfile, you would follow these steps:

1. Starting at Program Manager, open the Accessories group.

2. Click (once) the Cardfile icon to select it.

3. Choose **File ➤ Properties** from the Program Manager menu bar to get to the Program Item Properties dialog box for Cardfile.

4. In the Command Line portion of the dialog box, click the mouse pointer to the right of CARDFILE.EXE. Then press the space bar, type in the complete name of your card file, and choose OK. In Figure 9.1, I've specified mycards.crd as the name of the index card file to autoload.

FIGURE 9.1:

The Program Item Properties dialog box for the Cardfile applet modified so that it automatically loads cards stored in a file named mycards.crd.

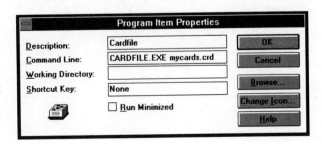

In the future, whenever you double-click the Cardfile icon, it will start with your index cards already loaded and ready for use.

You can use the same basic technique to autoload your appointments when you first start Calendar. Just type the name of your appointment file after CALENDAR.EXE in the Command Line box.

AUTOLOADING DOCUMENTS ON THE FLY

You probably won't want to autoload a specific document file into a general-purpose application, such as a word processor or spreadsheet. But there's still a shortcut you can take to load a document into an application without using File Manager or **File ➤ Open**. Just choose **File ➤ Run** in Program Manager, and enter the command used to start the application, followed by a space and the name of the document file. For example, Figure 9.2 shows how you'd fill in the Run dialog box to run Write and load singer.wri.

The startup command for an application is its filename, with or without the .exe extension.

If the application you want to run is not in the PATH statement of your autoexec.bat file, you'll need to include its path in the Run dialog box. Similarly, if the document you want to load is not in the current directory, include its path. For instance, to start WordPerfect for Windows, located on the c:\wpwin directory,

FIGURE 9.2:

The Run dialog box with instructions to run the Write applet and load the singer.wri document.

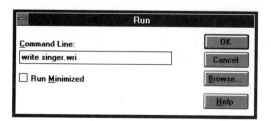

and load a file named myletter.wp, located on a directory named c:\wpwin\docs, you would enter this startup command in the Run dialog box:

c:\wpwin\wpwin.exe c:\wpwin\docs\myletter.wp

Of course, Windows was developed in part to make long program lines like the one above unnecessary; so you probably won't often use **File ➤ Run** when you need to specify that much detail.

If you prefer clicking to typing, remember that you can also load a document file into its associated application by double-clicking the name of the document file in File Manager.

AUTOSTARTING YOUR FAVORITE APPLICATIONS

You can have Windows *autostart* (automatically run) any application as soon as you start Windows. To do so, just Ctrl+drag a copy of the application's icon into the Startup group. For example, to have Windows automatically start Calendar, you would follow these steps:

1. If it isn't already open, open the application's group window (in this example, Accessories).

2. Move and size the window so you can see both the Startup group icon and open group window, as in Figure 9.3.

3. Move the mouse pointer to the Calendar icon.

Remember, if you don't hold down the Ctrl key while dragging an icon, that icon will be moved, rather than copied to the destination window.

4. Hold down the Ctrl key, then hold down the mouse button and drag a copy of the icon onto the Startup icon. Release first the mouse button, then the Ctrl key.

FIGURE 9.3:

The Accessories window open and positioned so that the Startup icon is visible in Program Manager. You can now copy Accessory icons onto the Startup icon.

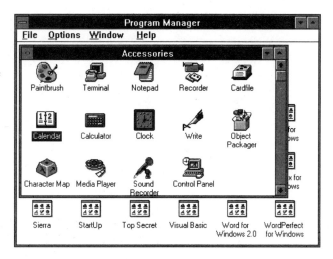

The Startup group should now contain a copy of the icon you dragged to it.

Of course, you can drag any other applications that you might want to start into the Startup group to autostart them.

STARTING AN APPLICATION AS AN ICON

You can always decide whether you want an application to start as an open window (the normal way), or just as a minimized icon. For example, the Clock accessory displays the current time even when it's minimized, so you don't need to open its window.

To start an application as an icon, you need to select the Run Minimized option in that application's Program Properties dialog box after placing it in the Startup group.

1. Click (once) on the application's icon in the Startup window.

2. Choose **File ➤ Properties** from the Program Manager menu bar.

3. Click the Run Minimized check box in the Program Item Properties dialog box, so it's marked with an X, and choose OK.

4. Close the Startup window.

5. If you need to tidy up, choose **Window ➤ Arrange Icons**, then (if you want to save the current desktop arrangement) hold down the Shift key and choose **File ➤ Exit Windows**.

To start any application as an icon from within Program Manager, just hold down the Shift key while double-clicking the application's icon.

If you want to test out your new configuration, choose **File ➤ Exit Windows** to get back to DOS. Then restart Windows with the usual **win** command at the DOS command prompt, and choose OK.

REMOVING AN ICON FROM STARTUP

If you decide you don't want to autostart a particular application anymore, just open the Startup group. Then click the application's icon and press Delete (Del) or choose **File ➤ Delete**. Then choose Yes when asked if you're sure.

THE BIGGER PICTURE

Windows has many other shortcuts you can use to get to a specific application or document more quickly. The remaining sections discuss some shortcuts that you might be able to tailor to your favorite applications.

SWITCHING AMONG APPLICATIONS WITH SHORTCUT KEYS

As you know, you can switch to any open application using the Alt+Tab keys, or Task Manager. If (like most users) you run Windows in 386 enhanced mode on a 386 or 486 computer, you can also define a shortcut key to take you directly to a specific open application.

When defining such shortcut keys, make sure each application uses a unique shortcut key. It's best to make a list of the keys you want to use, and to use Ctrl+Shift combinations, as these are rarely used as shortcut keys within a given application. And, if you use macros, avoid assigning the same shortcut keys to both a macro and an application. Once you've chosen the shortcut key for an application, use the application's Program Item Properties dialog box to assign the shortcut to the application. That is, open the application's group window, click on the application's icon, and choose **File ➤ Properties**. In the dialog box, click the Shortcut Key option, then press the shortcut keys you want to assign to that application. For instance, in Figure 9.4, I pressed Ctrl+Shift+A to assign that keystroke combination to Calendar.

After completing the dialog box, choose OK to return to Program Manager.

In the future, you can *start* the application using the shortcut key if (and only if) Program Manager is active when you press the shortcut key. The application's group need not be open. The real advantage is that once the application is started, and you've moved on to some other application, you can switch *back to* that open application using the shortcut key at any time.

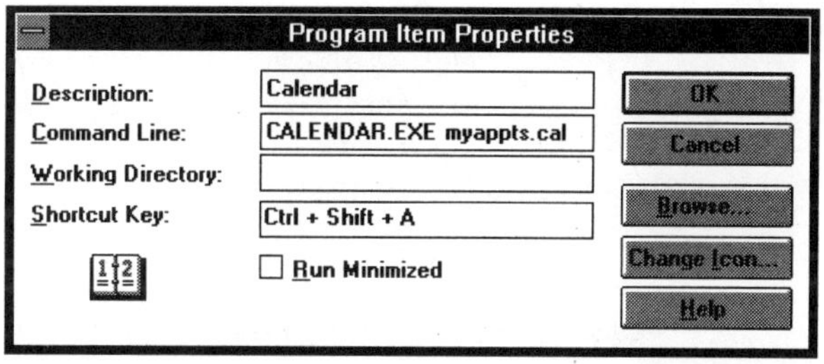

FIGURE 9.4:
The shortcut keystroke combination Ctrl+Shift+A assigned to the Calendar applet.

Program Item Properties	
Description:	Calendar
Command Line:	CALENDAR.EXE myappts.cal
Working Directory:	
Shortcut Key:	Ctrl + Shift + A
☐ Run Minimized	

OK / Cancel / Browse... / Change Icon... / Help

AUTOSTARTING APPLICATIONS ON THE FLY

Even if you don't put an application into the Startup group, you can still start it with Windows from the DOS command prompt. Simply follow the **win** command with a space and the name of the application you want to start.

For instance, to start Windows and Word for Windows, you would enter this DOS command:

```
win winword
```

If Word for Windows isn't in the PATH statement of your autoexec.bat file, and is located on the directory c:\winword, you'd need to include the path to the program, as below:

```
win c:\winword\winword
```

To load a document into an application you start with Windows, follow the application's command with a space and name of the document to open. For instance, to load Windows, Word for Windows, and a document named myletter.doc, you'd enter the command:

```
win c:\winword\winword myletter.doc
```

Again, you may need to include the path to the document in the command. For instance, this command tells Word for Windows to look for the file myletter.doc on the c:\letters directory:

```
win c:\winword\winword c:\letters\myletter.doc
```

BYPASSING THE SIGN-ON LOGO

You can bypass the sign-on logo simply by following your Windows startup command with a space and a colon (:). For instance:

```
win :
```

or

```
win c:\winword\winword c:\letters\myletter.doc :
```

BYPASSING THE STARTUP APPLICATIONS

If, for whatever reason, you want to prevent Windows from loading the applications in the Startup group when beginning a new session, just hold down the Shift key after typing the **win** command. Keep that Shift key depressed until you see the Windows desktop or a Windows application on your screen.

BYPASSING THE WIN COMMAND

If you'd prefer to have your computer start up with Windows rather than DOS in control, you can edit your autoexec.bat file to make **win** the last command in that file. Make sure you use a text editor, such as Notepad or the DOS 5 Edit editor, to make this change. Also make sure that **win** is the last command in the file. Otherwise, any commands that come after it won't be executed until after you exit Windows.

If you have any hesitation about tampering with autoexec.bat, you might want to skip this procedure and ask your local DOS guru for some assistance.

FOR MORE INFORMATION

For more information on the techniques introduced in this lesson, and related topics, see:

Applications

File Manager

Icons

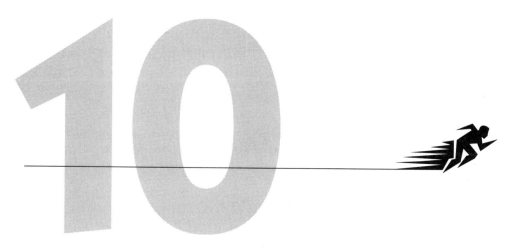

*E*XTRA GOODIES: MODEMS, SOUND, AND MULTIMEDIA

In this lesson we'll look at techniques for using optional hardware that you may have installed on your computer, particularly a modem, sound card, and CD-ROM drive.

USING YOUR MODEM

As you probably know, a modem is a device that lets you communicate with other computers via the phone lines. You can use your modem to link up to information services, such as Dow Jones News/Retrieval, electronic "bulletin boards," such as CompuServe, as well as other PCs. You can also copy files to and from these remote computers to your own computer.

STARTING TERMINAL

To use your modem, you need *communications software*. Terminal, which comes with Windows 3.1, will usually do the trick. Starting Terminal is an easy task:

1. Starting a Program Manager, double-click the Accessories group.

2. Double-click the Terminal icon.

Terminal's window appears as in Figure 10.1. The large blank area is where you'll do your communicating. You can size and move Terminal's window as you would any other.

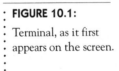
· **FIGURE 10.1:**
· Terminal, as it first
· appears on the screen.

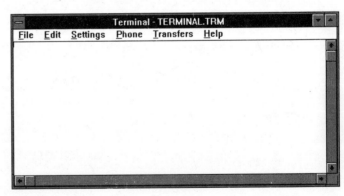

DEFINING COMMUNICATIONS SETTINGS

The first step to using your modem is to define the communications settings you'll need to link up with another computer. The most commonly used settings are no parity, 8 data bits, and 1 stop bit (usually abbreviated as N-8-1). A few services, such as BIX and CompuServe, require 7-E-1. Follow these steps to define communications settings:

1. From Terminal's menu bar, choose **Settings ➤ Communications**.

2. Choose the highest baud rate that both you and the computer you're communicating with can support. The most common baud rate is 2400, but 19200 is becoming more common.

3. To define the common N-8-1 settings, first choose 8 under Data Bits.

4. Under Stop Bits, choose 1.

5. Under Parity, choose None.

> *To communicate with CompuServe or another service that requires 7-E-1, set Data Bits to 7, Stop Bits to 1, and Parity to Even.*

6. Under Connector, choose the com (communications) port where you've plugged in your modem.

In most cases, you can leave the remaining options in the dialog box at their default settings: Flow Control set to Xon/Xoff, and Parity Check and Carrier Detect unselected. Figure 10.2 shows how the dialog box would look after choosing 2400, N-8-1, and COM 2 as the port that the modem is connected to.

FIGURE 10.2:
Communication dialog box configured for the common N-8-1 settings, 2400 baud, with the modem connected to com port 2.

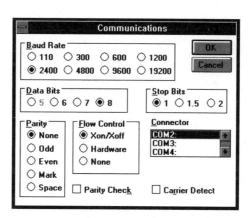

DEFINING THE PHONE NUMBER

Now you need to tell Terminal the phone number you want to dial out to:

1. First, choose OK to leave the Communications dialog box.

2. Choose **Settings ➤ Phone Number**.

3. Type the phone number for the other computer or service, just as you would dial it on a telephone, including any prefixes. If it takes a few seconds to get a dial tone after dialing the prefix, follow the prefix by a comma for each two seconds of delay you need. For instance, if you need to dial 9 to dial out, and need four seconds of delay, you'd type **9,,1-619-555-1234.**

4. Choose OK to leave the dialog box.

CHOOSING A BINARY TRANSFER PROTOCOL

If you plan on downloading (receiving) or uploading (sending) files, you'll need to choose a *protocol* for both parties to use. Terminal supports two widely used protocols; XModem/CRC and Kermit. The first of these is more common among bulletin boards, but the latter is faster.

Take the following steps to choose a protocol:

1. Choose **Settings ➤ Binary Transfers**. You'll see the dialog box shown in Figure 10.3.

2. Choose a protocol, then choose OK.

FIGURE 10.3:
For binary transfers, you can use either Xmodem or Kermit protocols.

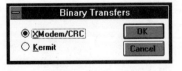

SAVING COMMUNICATIONS SETTINGS

Now, to save the settings so that you need not go though this rigmarole in the future:

1. Choose **File ➤ Save As**.

2. Type in an easily identifiable file name. Terminal will add the extension .trm to whatever file name you provide.

You can define as many communications (.trm) files as you wish. That way, you need only define the settings once. In the future, you just need to open the appropriate communications settings file, using **File ➤ Open** in Terminal, to call another computer.

CALLING ANOTHER COMPUTER

Once you've defined the communications settings, phone number, and binary transfer method, and saved all that information in a .trm file, you can use that file to call another computer:

1. Make sure your modem is ready, turned on, and correctly connected to the phone jack. If you're calling another PC user, that person should do the same.

2. Open Terminal, if you haven't done so already. Then choose **File ➤ Open** from Terminal's menu bar, and double-click the appropriate settings file for the person or service you want to call. If you're calling another PC, the recipient should have their communications software open with the same communications settings (e.g., 2400 N-8-1) in place.

The name of the currently selected communications settings file appears in Terminal's title bar.

3. If you're the person doing the calling, choose **Phone ➤ Dial**. If someone else is calling you, keep the Terminal window open, and just wait for the call to come through.

4. When the connection is made, the high pitched tone (if any) will stop, and you may see a message such as CONNECT 2400.

5. If you're *receiving* a call from another PC user, you should see RING on your screen when the call comes in. Type **ata** and press ↵ to put your phone into auto-answer mode at that point.

TIP
*If typing **ata** in response to RING doesn't answer the phone, see your modem manual or communications software documentation for more information on auto-answer.*

6. If nothing seems to happen after the connection is made, first press ↵ once or twice. What happens next depends on whom you're calling:

   ◆ If you're calling Compuserve via the compuserve network, you should see the prompt *Host Name:* after pressing ↵ once or twice. Type **cis** (for Compuserve Information Service), then press ↵. You'll then be prompted for your Compuserve user ID. See your Compuserve documentation for instructions on proceeding.

   ◆ If you're calling another PC, you should be able to communicate at this point by simply typing messages to one another, following each message you type with a couple of ↵ keystrokes.

If you have any problems, see "Communications Troubleshooting" later in this lesson.

DOWNLOADING FILES FROM AN INFORMATION SERVICE

If you're communicating with an information service, and want to download a file to your computer, that service will provide downloading instructions.

Once you begin the download, you may be asked for a protocol. From the service's menu of options, choose the protocol you defined earlier. When told to begin your transfer procedure, choose **Transfers ➤ Receive Binary File** from Terminal's menu bar. Choose the drive and directory where you want to store the incoming file, and provide a file name (it need not be the same as the file name you're downloading). Choose OK. After a brief delay, you should see the Bytes count at the bottom of Terminal's window keeping you informed of the progress (glance ahead to Figure 10.4 for an example).

The files you download from an information service may be compressed, and will need to be decompressed before you can use them. See your service bureau's documentation, or contact the information service, for more information on decompressing files.

TRANSFERRING FILES WITH ANOTHER PC

If you're communicating with another PC, and can type messages back and forth, you're connected and ready to transfer files. Here's how:

1. If you're the person sending the file, choose **Transfers ➤ Send Binary File**. Choose the drive and directory location of the file that you want to send, then click the name of the file.

2. If you're receiving the file, choose **Transfers ➤ Receive Binary File**. Choose any drive and directory to store the incoming file on, and give it any name you wish. Choose OK after finishing your entries.

If you plan on transferring files often, consider purchasing file compression software, such as the widely used shareware program PKZIP. Compressed files transfer more reliably, and up to 75% faster.

When both users have given the OK, the transfer begins. The sender will see progress in an odometer at the bottom of Terminal's window. (It may take a couple of minutes to see any progress if you're sending a large file.) The receiver sees progress being made in bytes, as Figure 10.4.

FIGURE 10.4:
Sender and recipient progress reports at the bottom of the Terminal window during a file transfer.

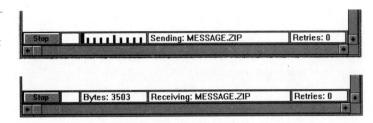

If it's going to take a while to complete the transfer, you can run other applications, as long as you don't close Terminal's window. Your best bet might be to size and move Terminal's window so you can keep an eye on its progress while you work in other applications.

COMMUNICATIONS TROUBLESHOOTING

Here are some common problems and their solutions:

- **Can't dial out:** Make sure the Line jack on the modem is connected to the wall jack (not the telephone itself). If you have an external modem, make sure it's turned on and ready to go, and connected to the correct serial port. In Terminal, choose **Settings ➤ Communications**, and make sure the correct port for your modem is selected under the Connector option.

- **Text is garbled on the screen**: Make sure that sender and receiver are using the same communications settings (baud rate, data bits, stop bits, and parity) under **Settings ➤ Communications**.

- **Text on the screen is too small to read:** Choose **Settings ➤ Terminal Preferences**. Under the Terminal Font option, choose a different typeface and perhaps a larger size.

- **Everything you type is doubled:** Choose **Settings ➤ Terminal Preferences** and deselect the Local Echo option under Terminal Modes.

- **Can't see what you're typing on the screen:** This is normal when entering a password. But if it persists, choose **Settings ➤ Terminal Preferences**, then select Local Echo under Terminal Modes.

- **Pressing ↵ doesn't move cursor to the next line**: Choose **Settings ➤ Terminal Preferences**. Under CR -> CR/LF, choose the Inbound and Outbound options.

- **Text is cut off at the right edge of the window:** Enlarge (or maximize) Terminal's window. Or choose **Settings ➤ Terminal Preferences**, make sure **80** is selected under Columns, and, if necessary, choose a smaller point size under the Terminal Font option.

- **Can't Send/Receive Files**: If you're sending a file, be sure to choose **Send** *Binary* File (rather than *Text* file). If you're receiving a file, make sure to choose **Receive** *Binary* File (rather than *Text* file.) Make sure both sender and receiver are using the same protocol under **Settings ➤ Binary Transfers**.

DISCONNECTING FROM A REMOTE COMPUTER

It's important to remember that the modem does not automatically hang up the phone when you've finished communicating with another user. So to hang up and put your phone back on the hook:

1. If you're communicating with an information service or bulletin board, log off as per instructions for that service. For instance, to log off from Compuserve, you type **bye** at any ! prompt, then press ↵.

2. Choose **Phone ➤ Hangup** from Terminal's menu bar.

When you've hung up the phone and finished with Terminal, you can close it as you would any other application:

1. Choose **File ➤ Exit** or double-click Terminal's Control-Menu box.

2. If you made any changes to the current communications settings, you'll be asked about saving those changes. Choose Yes to save your current settings.

FUN WITH SOUNDS

If you have a sound card, you can use Windows' Sound Recorder to play, record, and experiment with sounds. Before Sound Recorder will work, however, you must install the sound card, install the software required to operate the card, and install the Windows 3.1 drivers for the card, as per the manufacturer's instructions. Also check the sound card's documentation for information on controlling the volume and settings, particularly if you have any problems with Sound Recorder.

STARTING SOUND RECORDER

To start Sound Recorder:

1. Open the Accessories group (if it isn't already open).
2. Double-click the Sound Recorder icon.

You'll see Sound Recorder, as in Figure 10.5. The roles of various buttons in Sound Recorder are also illustrated in the figure.

· FIGURE 10.5:
· Sound Recorder as it
· first appears on your
· screen.

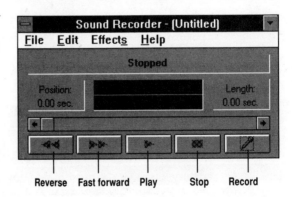

PLAYING A SOUND

To play a sound using Sound Recorder:

1. Choose **File ➤ Open** from Sound Recorder's menu bar.

150

2. In the dialog box that appears, double-click the name of the .wav sound file you want to play. The name of the current sound file appears in the title bar.

3. Click the Play button.

Here are some fun things to experiment with while you've got the sound file in Sound Recorder (just click the Play button after choosing menu options to hear their effects):

*   Choose **Effects ➤ Increase Volume (by 25%)** to increase the volume. Or choose **Effects ➤ Decrease Volume** to decrease the volume.

*   Choose **Effects ➤ Increase Speed (by 100%)** to double the playback speed, or choose **Effects ➤ Decrease Speed** to slow down the play-back speed.

*   Choose **Effects ➤ Add Echo** to add some echo to the sound. Each time you choose this option, you add some more echo.

*   Choose **Effects ➤ Reverse** to hear the sound backwards.

After experimenting with the sound, you can use **File ➤ Save** to replace the old file with your modified version, **File ➤ Save As** to save the new version with a different name, or **File ➤ New** to abandon your changes.

RECORDING A SOUND

To record a sound, you first need to plug a microphone into the sound card, as per the manufacturer's instructions. (Also check the manufacturer's documentation for information on setting the recording level; if it is turned all the way down, Sound Recorder won't pick up the sound.) When you're ready to record:

1. If you already have a sound file loaded, choose **File ➤ New** to start with a new (Untitled) sound.

2. Click the Record button, then speak (or play) the sound you want to record, up to a minute, or whatever your system's memory will provide for.

> As a point of reference, one minute of recorded speech typically occupies about one megabyte.

3. Click the Stop button to stop recording.

4. To hear the recorded sound, click the Play button.

5. If you want to add special effects, try the various options on the Effects menu described in the previous section.

6. To save the recorded sound, choose **File ➤ Save** and provide a file name. (Recorder will add the extension .wav to whatever file name you provide.)

If you have any problems recording, first make sure the microphone is properly connected to the microphone jack on the sound card. Then check your sound card documentation to see if you need to make any special adjustments.

USING MEDIA PLAYER

Media Player is Windows' general-purpose multimedia device player. It can play both wave (.wav) files and MIDI Musical Instrument Digital Interface) files, as well as any MCI (Media Control Interface) multimedia device attached to your computer, such as audio and video disc players.

Before you can use Media Player to play such a device, you must install the device, its software, and the Windows 3.1 drivers, as per the manufacturer's instructions.

STARTING MEDIA PLAYER

To start Media Player:

1. Open the Accessories group (if it isn't already open).

2. Double-click the Media Player icon.

Media Player appears, as in Figure 10.6.

FIGURE 10.6:

Media Player, with various buttons identified.

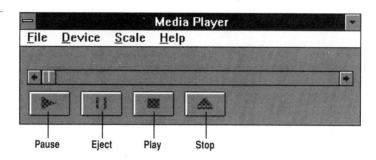

PLAYING A MIDI FILE

If you have a sound card that supports MIDI, and have installed the driver, you can follow these steps to play a MIDI file:

1. Choose **Device ➤ MIDI Sequencer**.

2. From the Open dialog box that appears, choose the drive and directory that the MIDI file is stored on, the double-click the name of the MIDI file.

3. Click the Play button.

To stop playing the MIDI file at any time, just click the Stop button.

PLAYING SOUND FILES

If you have a sound card, you can also use Media Player to play wave (.wav) files. To do so, choose **Device ➤ Sound**. Then double-click the name of the wave file you want to hear, and click the Play button.

LISTENING TO YOUR FAVORITE CDS

If you have a CD-ROM drive, you can use Media Player to listen to standard audio CDs (the same ones you use in your stereo), perhaps while running other Windows applications. To do so, insert the CD into the CD-ROM drive, choose **Device ➤ CD Audio**, click the Play button, and enjoy!

To listen to a specific song, just drag the scroll box to the song's track number. Use the Pause, Play, Stop, and Eject buttons just as you would on an audio CD player.

THE BIGGER PICTURE

If you have multimedia devices attached to your computer, or are planning to get some, here are some additional things you can do.

RECORDING WITHOUT A MICROPHONE

If you have a CD-ROM drive in your computer, and you purchase and install multimedia "mixer" software, you can record from an audio CD directly to sound files without a microphone. This is a great way to copy sound effects from CDs to wave files (keep in mind that you can't *distribute* copyrighted sounds without permission from the copyright holder). For instance, Figure 10.7 shows Sound Recorder and Media Player on the screen. Between them, Pocket Mixer, from Media Vision's Multimedia Upgrade kit, is configured to record sounds from the CD directly to sound files.

USING CD-ROM DISKS

Of course, if you have a CD-ROM drive, you'll want to use it to play multimedia CDs as well as audio CDs. However, you don't use Media Player to do so. Instead, you install the software on the disk under Windows, and then run it from Program Manager like any other application. You'll have full access to the sounds, voice, graphics, and animations on the CD. Figure 10.8 shows Compton's Multimedia Encyclopedia, which uses standard Windows interface elements and its own button bar.

FIGURE 10.7:

Media Vision's Pocket Mixer, shown here between Windows' Media Player and Sound Recorder, lets you record from a CD or other source to a sound file without a microphone.

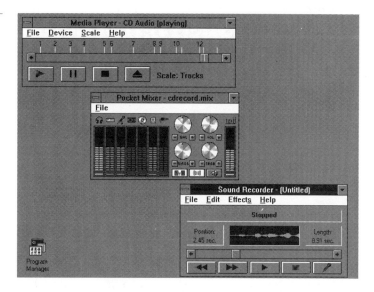

FIGURE 10.8:

A sample "page" from Compton's Multimedia Encyclopedia, with text, sound effects, graphics, and animation available through a typical Windows interface.

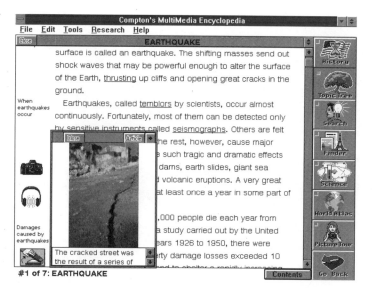

FOR MORE INFORMATION

See the following Reference entries for more information about topics introduced in this lesson:

Media Player

Sound Recorder

Terminal

PART II

ALPHABETICAL REFERENCE

386 ENHANCED MODE

386 enhanced mode gives Windows the effect of having more memory than is physically available on the computer, by using available disk space as *virtual memory*. 386 Enhanced mode also lets you run more than one non-Windows (DOS) application at a time.

If you have an 80386 or higher microprocessor with at least 640K of conventional memory and 1024K of extended memory (2MB total RAM), Windows *automatically* uses 386 enhanced mode.

If your computer has an 80286 microprocessor, or an 80386 with less than 640K conventional and 384K extended memory (1MB), you cannot use 386 enhanced mode. If your computer has less than 2MB of memory, it will probably run more slowly in 386 enhanced mode than in standard mode.

TO FORCE WINDOWS TO RUN IN 386 ENHANCED MODE

◆ Type **win /3** and press ↵ at the DOS prompt.

TO FIND OUT WHAT MODE YOUR COMPUTER IS USING

◆ Choose **Help ➤ About** from the Program Manager menus, or from the menu of any running applet.

See Also Applications; PIF Editor

APPLICATIONS

In Windows, the term *application* refers to any program you run in the operating environment. From Windows, you can run both Windows applications and non-Windows (DOS) applications.

TO START AN APPLICATION FROM PROGRAM MANAGER

1. Open the Program Manager window if it's not already open.

2. Open the group window containing the application if it's not already open.

3. Double-click the icon of the application you want to run.

TO START AN APPLICATION FROM FILE MANAGER

1. Double-click the File Manager icon in the Program Manager's Main group.

2. Click the drive icon you want.

3. Click the directory icon you want.

4. Double-click the filename of the program file, or of a document file that is *associated* with a particular application (see the File Manager entry).

TO START AN APPLICATION USING RUN

1. Choose **File ➤ Run** from the Program Manager.

2. Type the complete path name of the program file, or choose the Browse button and double-click the name of the file you want.

3. If you want to reduce the application to an icon when it starts, select the **Run Minimized** check box.

4. Choose OK.

TO SWITCH BETWEEN APPLICATIONS

- ◆ If the application's window is visible, click in that window; or, if the application is running as an icon, double-click the icon.
- ◆ Or press Alt+Tab to return to the application you last used.
- ◆ Or press and hold the Alt key while pressing Tab repeatedly. Each time you press Tab, you'll see the title of an open application. When you see the title you want, release the keys.
- ◆ Or press Alt+Esc repeatedly to cycle through open application windows and icons until you reach the one you want.
- ◆ Or press Ctrl+Esc to open the Task List, then double-click the name of the application you want.

TO TOGGLE A NON-WINDOWS APPLICATION BETWEEN A WINDOW AND A FULL SCREEN

- ◆ Press Alt+↵. (Press Alt+↵ again to return to the previous appearance.)

NOTE Only non-Windows applications running in 386 enhanced mode can be toggled in this way. Non-Windows applications always run in a full screen in standard mode.

TO QUIT A WINDOWS APPLICATION

- ◆ Choose **File ➤ Exit** from the application's menu bar.
  Or double-click the application's Control-Menu box.
- ◆ Or press Alt+F4.
- ◆ Or press Ctrl+Esc to open the Task List, select the application name, then choose the End Task button.

NOTE If you haven't saved changes to the document you're working on, you'll be prompted to save them.

TO QUIT A NON-WINDOWS APPLICATION

- Choose the application's usual command for exiting or quitting the program.

See Also Lesson 9; Control Menu; File Manager; PIF Editor; Task List; Windows; Windows Setup

CALCULATOR

The Windows Calculator operates as both a *standard calculator*, for simple calculations, and a *scientific calculator*, for advanced scientific, programming, and statistical calculations. You can use the Clipboard to copy calculation results to other applications or to paste calculations from another application to Calculator using the standard **Edit ➤ Copy** and **Edit ➤ Paste** commands.

TO START CALCULATOR

◆ Double-click the Calculator icon in the Accessories group of Program Manager.

EXAMPLE The standard calculator appears below:

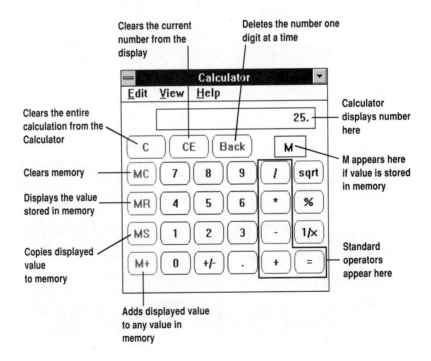

The scientific calculator appears below:

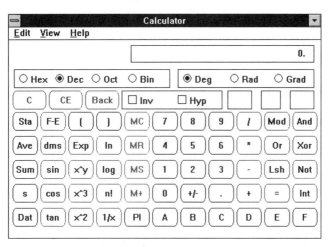

NOTE The first time you choose Calculator, you'll see the standard calculator. The next time you choose it, you'll see whichever calculator you used last.

TO SWITCH BETWEEN CALCULATORS

◆ Choose **View** from the menu bar, then choose either **Scientific** or **Standard**.

NOTE The numbers on your numeric keypad work only when the Num Lock key is turned on (as indicated by its keyboard light).

TO MAKE CORRECTIONS

Choose one of the buttons (or press a key) listed below:

BUTTON	KEY	PURPOSE
Back	Backspace	Deletes one digit at a time from the display area.
CE	[None]	Clears all the digits in the display area.
C	Esc	Clears the entire calculation.

See Also Lesson 4; Clipboard

CALENDAR

The Calendar applet provides a planning calendar in either month-at-a-glance or daily appointment book format. You can also use it to set an alarm to remind you of important appointments.

Calendar uses the date and time settings from your computer.

TO START CALENDAR

- ◆ Double-click the Calendar icon in the Accessories group of Program Manager. Initially, Calendar appears in Day view.

EXAMPLE Here's a calendar for November 9, 1992 in Day view. Alarms are set at 12:00 noon and 4:15 PM.

Click the buttons to switch
to the previous or next day

Double-click the date
to switch to Month view

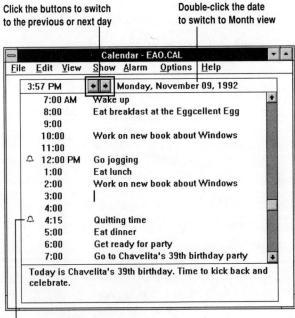

The bell icon shows where we've
set an alarm by pressing F5

Here's the same calendar in Month view. The 9th and 18th are marked dates.

Click the buttons to switch to the previous or next month

Double-click the date to switch to Day view

```
┌─────────────────────────────────────────────────┐
│ ─        Calendar - EA0.CAL              ▼ ▲     │
├─────────────────────────────────────────────────┤
│ File  Edit  View  Show  Alarm  Options  Help     │
├─────────────────────────────────────────────────┤
│ 3:58 PM      ◄ ►  Monday, November 09, 1992      │
│                    November 1992                  │
│   S      M      T      W      T      F      S     │
│   1      2      3      4      5      6      7     │
│   8     [9]    10     11     12     13     14     │
│  15     16     17     18     19     20     21     │
│  22     23     24     25     26     27     28     │
│  29     30                                        │
│  Today is Chavelita's 39th birthday. Time to kick │
│  back and celebrate.                              │
└─────────────────────────────────────────────────┘
```

TO SWITCH BETWEEN
THE DAILY AND MONTHLY DISPLAY

◆ Choose **View ➤ Day** (or press F8) or **View ➤ Month** (or press F9), respectively.

Shortcut: Double-click the month, day, and year area near the top of the calendar (next to the → button). Or double-click the selected date in Month view.

TO VIEW INFORMATION FOR A SPECIFIC DATE

Choose one of these options from the Show menu:

◆ **Today**: Today's information.

◆ **Previous** (or press Ctrl+PgUp): Previous month (in Month view) or the previous day (in Day view).

- **Next**: Next month (in Month view) or the next day (in Day view).
- **Date** (or press F4): Specified date. Type the date you want, then choose OK.

NOTE Date entries must be between January 1, 1980 and December 31, 2099. For dates outside the twentieth century, you must type all four digits of the year.

TO VIEW A DIFFERENT DATE USING YOUR MOUSE

In Month view, click the ← and → buttons at the top of the calendar to switch to previous or following months, then click the date you want. In Day view, clicking the ← or → buttons switches to the previous or following day.

TO ENTER APPOINTMENTS

1. In Day view, move the insertion point to the appointment time you want. To schedule an appointment for a time not displayed (e.g., 3:30), you must add a special time (see below).
2. Type up to 80 characters of text.

TO ADD A NOTE
OR REMINDER FOR A SPECIFIC DATE

In Month or Day view, select a date. Then type up to three lines of text in the scratch pad area at the bottom of the calendar. The text will automatically wrap when it reaches the right border of the scratch pad.

TO SET AN ALARM

Switch to Day view, then do one of the following:

- To set the alarm, move the insertion point to the appointment time you want, then choose **Alarm ➤ Set** or press F5. Repeat these steps to remove an alarm from an appointment.

◆ To set all alarms to go off up to 10 minutes early, choose **Alarm ➤ Controls**, type a number from 0 to 10 in the Early Ring box, then choose OK. Set the Early Ring back to 0 to disable early alarms.

NOTE The alarm will sound only if the Calendar is open (or minimized) when it's time to sound the alarm. To turn off the alarm when it sounds, switch to the Calendar window or restore the Calendar icon. Then choose OK from the Alarm dialog box.

TO CONTROL THE TIME INTERVAL, HOUR FORMAT, AND STARTING TIME

◆ Choose **Options ➤ Day Settings**, select the options you want to use, then choose OK.

NOTE Options are:

◆ **Interval** (intervals between daily appointments).

◆ **Hour Format** (12 or 24-hour clock).

◆ **Starting Time** (time that appears at the upper-left of the Calendar window when you first view an appointment day).

TO ADD OR DELETE A SPECIAL TIME NOT DISPLAYED

1. In Day view, choose **Options ➤ Special Time** (or press F7).
2. Type the time you want in the Special Time box.
3. Select AM or PM if you're using a 12-hour clock (as specified by the Date/Time settings of Control Panel).
4. Choose the Insert button if you want to insert this special time, or the Delete button to delete this time.

TO MARK OR UNMARK A DATE

1. In Day or Month view, select the date you want to mark.

2. Choose **Options ➤ Mark**.

3. To mark the date, select one or more options for the symbol you want to use. To unmark the date, remove the "X" from all the check box options.

4. Choose OK.

NOTE Dates appear marked in Month view only. You can use different symbols for holidays, paydays, birthdays, and so forth.

TO REMOVE APPOINTMENT DAY ENTRIES

1. Choose **File ➤ Open** to open the file you want to remove appointments from, and specify the file name.

2. Choose **Edit ➤ Remove**.

3. In the From box, type the first date you want to remove appointments from.

4. In the To box, type the last date you want to remove appointments from. Or leave the To box blank to remove only one day's appointments.

5. Choose OK.

TO PRINT APPOINTMENTS

1. Choose **File ➤ Print**.

2. In the From box, type the first date you want to print.

3. In the To box, type the last date you want to print. Or leave the To box blank to print only one day's appointments.

4. Choose OK.

TO SAVE CHANGES TO AN APPOINTMENT CALENDAR

- ◆ Choose **File ➤ Save**. If this is the first time you've saved the file, specify a file name, then choose OK.

See Also Date and Time; International

CARDFILE

Cardfile is an electronic index card file that you can use to store any information to which you want quick access. If you have a Hayes or Hayes-compatible modem connected to your computer, you can also use Cardfile to make a phone call.

TO START CARDFILE

- ◆ Double-click the Cardfile icon in the Accessories group of Program Manager.

TO ADD A NEW CARD

1. Choose **Card ➤ Add** or press F7.
2. Type the text that identifies the contents of this card (up to 39 characters), then choose OK.
3. Type the text for each line of the card (up to 40 characters per line). Text lines will wrap when your typing reaches the right edge of the card.

NOTE Cards are maintained in sorted order based on the index line at the top of the card. If you want to use Cardfile to dial telephone numbers, enter long-distance phone numbers in the form *x-(xxx)xxx-xxxx* (e.g., *1-(800)555-1212*). Enter local calls in the form xxx-xxxx (e.g., *555-1212*).

TO SWITCH BETWEEN LIST VIEW AND CARD VIEW

Choose **View** ➤ **List**. To return to Card view, choose **View** ➤ **Card**.

NOTE List view is handy for moving quickly through the card file. You must switch back to Card view if you want to add text or pictures to the information area of the card.

TO MOVE THROUGH THE CARDS

- ◆ Click the right or left arrow in the status bar at the top of the Cardfile window.
- ◆ Or click on the index line of the card you want.
- ◆ Or choose **Search** ➤ **Go To** (or press F4), type just as much of the index line as you need to identify the card, then choose OK.
- ◆ Or use any of the keyboard shortcuts listed below.

PRESS	TO
PgDn	Scroll forward one card in Card view or forward one page of index lines in List view.
PgUp	Scroll backward one card in Card view or backward one page of index lines in List view.
Ctrl+Home	Bring the first card to the front.
Ctrl+End	Bring the last card to the front.
↓	Scroll one card forward in List view.
↑	Scroll one card backward in List view.
Ctrl+Shift+l	(where l is the first letter of the index line text) Scroll to first card with the specified letter in its index line.

TO FIND A CARD CONTAINING
TEXT THAT'S NOT ON AN INDEX LINE

1. Select the card where you want to begin the search.

2. Choose **Search ➤ Find**. The Find dialog box appears.

3. Type the text you want to find in the Find What text box.

4. If you want to match the capitalization exactly, select the Match Case check box.

5. Select the search direction (Up or Down).

6. Choose the Find Next button.

7. Repeat Step 6 as needed to locate the card you're looking for. Or, close the Find dialog box, then press F3 as needed to search for the text without displaying the dialog box.

TO ADD A PICTURE
OR OTHER OBJECT TO THE CURRENT CARD

1. In the picture's source application, use standard cut-and-paste or OLE techniques to copy the picture you want to the Clipboard.

2. Return to Cardfile, bring the card you want to the forefront, then choose **Edit ➤ Picture**.

3. Choose **Edit ➤ Paste** or **Edit ➤ Picture** to paste the picture. The picture will appear at the upper left-hand corner or at the bottom of the card.

4. If text exists on the card, the picture may cover it. Drag the picture to where you want it to appear.

5. To work with text on the card again, choose **Edit ➤ Text**.

NOTE Whenever you want to work with a picture or other object, you must first choose **Edit ➤ Picture**. To switch back to working with text, always choose **Edit ➤ Text**.

TO EDIT THE
CURRENT CARD (OR CREATE A NEW ONE)

- To edit the index line, double-click the index line, or press F6, or choose **Edit ➤ Index**. Type or change the index line entry (if desired), then choose OK.

- To edit text in the information area, make sure **Edit ➤ Text** is selected, then just click in that part of the card and use normal Windows editing techniques.

- Or to edit a picture or object, make sure **Edit ➤ Picture** is selected, then drag the picture (if you want to move it), or double-click the picture if you used OLE to place the picture on the card.

To undo changes made to a card, choose **Edit ➤ Restore**.

TO COPY THE CURRENT CARD TO A NEW CARD

- Choose **Card ➤ Duplicate**.

TO DELETE THE CURRENT CARD

- Choose **Card ➤ Delete**, then choose OK to confirm the deletion.

TO PRINT CARDS

- Choose **File ➤ Print** to print the current card, or choose **File ➤ Print All** to print all the cards.

TO DIAL A
PHONE NUMBER ON THE CURRENT CARD

1. If the phone number appears below any other numbers on the card, select the entire phone number you want to dial.

2. Choose **Card ➤ Autodial** or press F5. The Autodial dialog box appears.

3. If you need to set up your modem for dialing, choose the Setup>> button, fill in the setup options, then choose OK.

4. If you need to use a prefix, check the Use Prefix box. If you need to change the prefix, type the new prefix into the Prefix text box.

5. Choose OK to begin dialing.

6. When you hear ringing over your modem, pick up your telephone receiver and choose OK.

EXAMPLE Here's a sample Autodial dialog box after choosing the Setup>> button.

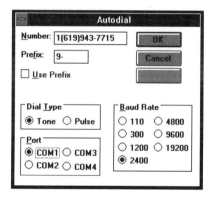

See Also Clipboard; Cut and Paste; Object Linking and Embedding; Object Packager; Paintbrush

CHARACTER MAP

The Character Map applet lets you insert special characters not found on the keyboard into Windows applications.

TO INSERT ONE OR
MORE CHARACTERS INTO A DOCUMENT

1. Open the application and document where you want to insert the special character(s).

2. Using whatever techniques the current application requires, choose the font that includes the character you want.

3. Switch to Program Manager and double-click Character Map in the Accessories group.

4. If the font displayed in the Character Map dialog box isn't the same as the font selected in your document, choose a font from the Font drop-down list.

5. Move the mouse pointer to a character, then press and hold down the left mouse button to see an enlarged picture of the character. Or, press Tab to position the cursor on the character you want, then press an arrow key to see an enlarged picture (to see another enlarged character, simply press another arrow key).

6. Double-click the character to copy it into the Characters to Copy box, or choose the Select button.

7. Repeat Steps 4 and 5 as many times as you want.

8. Choose the Copy button to copy the characters from the Characters to Copy box to the Clipboard.

9. Choose Close to close the Character Map, or just switch to your application window if you want to leave Character Map open.

10. Choose **Edit ➤ Paste** from the application's menu.

Shortcut: As an alternative to going through Character Map, you can type a special character by holding down the Alt key and, *using the numeric keypad*, typing the character's three- or four-digit number (as shown inside the back cover of this book).

NOTE If the special characters don't look right in the current document, select them and use the application's techniques to choose the appropriate TrueType font for the current characters. The font selected in the application must match the Character Map font.

See Also Lesson 5; Special Characters table (inside back cover); Clipboard; Cut and Paste; Fonts; Selecting Text and Graphics

CLIPBOARD

The Clipboard provides temporary storage for information you want to transfer (cut and paste) between applications and is always available when Windows is running. Information you cut or copy to the Clipboard remains there until you clear the Clipboard, cut or copy something new into it, or exit Windows. The Clipboard is also used for object linking and embedding. The Clipboard Viewer lets you view the current contents of the Clipboard.

TO VIEW THE CLIPBOARD CONTENTS

◆ Double-click Clipboard Viewer in the Main group of Program Manager.

EXAMPLE Here the Clipboard contains some graphics.

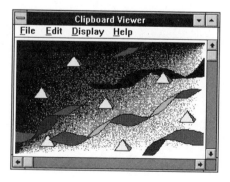

TO CLEAR THE CLIPBOARD CONTENTS

- While in the Clipboard Viewer, you can press the Delete key or choose **Edit ➤ Delete** to delete the current Clipboard contents.

See Also Applications; Cut and Paste; Drives, Directories and Files; Object Linking and Embedding

CLOCK

The Clock applet displays an analog or digital clock.

TO START CLOCK

- Double-click the Clock icon in the Accessories group of Program Manager.

NOTE When you start Clock for the first time, you'll see the standard analog clock. The clock always reflects the system date and time, with dates and times displayed in the current International format.

TO CUSTOMIZE THE CLOCK'S APPEARANCE

- Choose options from the Settings menu.

NOTE Options on the Settings menu are listed below:

OPTION	EFFECT
Analog	Switches to an analog clock display.
Digital	Switches to a digital clock display.
Set Font	Lets you change the font of the digital clock.

OPTION	EFFECT
No title	Removes the Settings menu from the display. To Redisplay the Settings menu, double-click anywhere in the Clock window, or press Esc.
Seconds	Adds or removes the second hand (analog) or seconds number (digital) from the Clock display. When this option is checked, seconds appear.
Date	Adds or removes the date from the clock display. When this option is checked, the date appears.

TO KEEP THE CLOCK ON TOP OF OTHER OPEN WINDOWS

◆ Click the Clock's Control-Menu box and check the **Always on Top** option. Remove the check mark to allow the clock to be covered by open windows.

See Also Control Menu; Date and Time; Fonts; International

CONTROL MENU

Most windows, icons, and dialog boxes have a Control menu at the upper-left corner for manipulating windows and switching to other applications. Control menus contain some combination of the following options:

Restore: Restores a window to its previous size.

Move: Lets you move the window using the arrow keys (press ↵ after positioning the outline image of the window).

Size: Lets you size the window using the arrow keys (press ↵ after positioning the outline image of the window).

Minimize: Reduces the window to an icon.

Maximize: Expands the window to full-screen size.

Close: Closes the window or dialog box.

Switch To: Opens the Task List dialog box, which lets you switch to another running application and rearrange windows.

Next: Switches to the next open document window or icon, if there is one.

The Control menu for a non-Windows application running in 386 enhanced mode includes these additional options:

Edit: Displays a cascading menu with additional editing commands (Mark, Copy, Paste, and Scroll) that are used primarily to transfer information to and from the Clipboard.

Settings: Displays a dialog box requesting information about multitasking options (Display mode, Tasking Options, Priority, and Special).

Fonts: Displays a dialog box for specifying the screen font for a DOS application.

TO OPEN THE CONTROL MENU FOR A WINDOWS APPLICATION

- Click the Control-Menu box in an open window, or the icon of a minimized window.

- Or press Alt+Spacebar for an application window, application icon, or dialog box.

- Or press Alt+- (hyphen) for a document window or document icon.

Shortcuts: To close a window, double-click the Control-Menu box. To close a dialog box *without* saving changes, double-click the Control-Menu box or press the Esc key.

TO OPEN THE CONTROL MENU FOR A NON-WINDOWS APPLICATION RUNNING IN STANDARD MODE

- ◆ Press Alt+Esc until you select the icon for the application, then click the icon or press Alt+Spacebar.

See Also Clipboard; Dialog Boxes; Icons; Keyboard Shortcuts; Menus; Task List; Windows

CUT AND PASTE

Cutting deletes the selected information from the document and places it on the Clipboard. *Copying* makes a duplicate of the selected information (without changing the document) and places it on the Clipboard. The methods for cutting and copying depend on whether you're using a Windows or non-Windows application.

TO CUT OR COPY INFORMATION TO THE CLIPBOARD (WINDOWS APPLICATION)

1. Select the information (text and/or graphics) you want to cut or copy.
2. Choose **Edit ➤ Cut** or **Edit ➤ Copy**.

Shortcuts: Press Shift+Del to cut selected information or Ctrl+Ins to copy selected information to the Clipboard.

TO COPY INFORMATION TO THE CLIPBOARD (NON-WINDOWS APPLICATION)

1. If the application is running in a full screen, press Alt+↵ to run it in a window.
2. Click on the application's Control-Menu box.

3. Choose **Edit ➤ Mark** from the Control menu.

4. Select the information you want to copy.

5. Press ↵ (or choose **Edit ➤ Copy** from the Control menu).

TO PASTE INFORMATION FROM THE CLIPBOARD (WINDOWS APPLICATION)

- Position the insertion point where you want the information to appear, then choose **Edit ➤ Paste** (or press Shift+Ins).

TO PASTE INFORMATION FROM THE CLIPBOARD (NON-WINDOWS APPLICATION)

Position the insertion point where you want the information to appear, then do one of the following:

- If the application is running in a window, open its Control menu and choose **Edit ➤ Paste**.

- If the application is running in a full screen, press Alt+Spacebar to open the Control menu, then choose **Paste** (in standard mode) or **Edit ➤ Paste** (in 386 enhanced mode).

NOTE If your application uses Alt+Spacebar for another purpose, use this method to open the Control menu: press Alt+Esc until you've selected the application's icon, then click the icon.

If you mark text that you want to copy in a DOS application, then receive an error message when you try to put that application back into full screen mode, first choose OK to cancel the error message. Then press Esc to "unmark" selected text, and try again.

See Also Applications; Clipboard; Control Menu; Print Screen; Selecting Text and Graphics

DATE AND TIME

The Date/Time option in Control Panel lets you reset the system date and time. The date and time formats used by Windows applications depend on the International settings.

TO CHANGE THE SYSTEM DATE OR TIME

1. Double-click the Control Panel icon in the Main group of Program Manager, then double-click the Date/Time icon.

2. Select the part of the date or time that you want to change:

   ◆ In the Date box, you can change the day, month, and/or year.

   ◆ In the Time box, you can change the hour, minute, seconds, or AM/PM suffix.

3. Type the new value, or click the arrow buttons at the right of the Date or Time box to change the selected part by one date or time unit at a time.

4. Choose OK to return to the Control Panel.

EXAMPLE The Date & Time dialog box appears below.

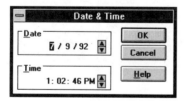

See Also International

DIALOG BOXES

Windows and its applications use dialog boxes to request more information from you or to supply information to you.

TO MOVE AROUND IN A DIALOG BOX

- Click the option you want. Or press Tab (to move forward) or Shift+Tab (to move backward) to the option you want. After moving to the option, you can select it or fill it in, as described in the following sections.

Shortcuts: Hold down the Alt key while typing the underlined letter in the option or button name. This shortcut selects or deselects a check box option and chooses a command button.

EXAMPLE A sample dialog box appears below:

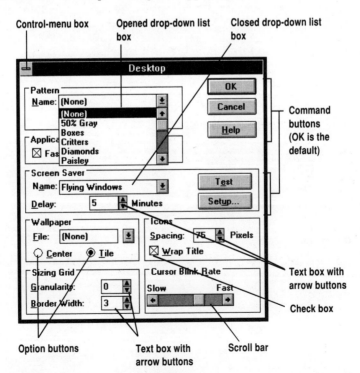

NOTE An option or button that's dimmed is unavailable at the moment, usually because it doesn't make sense in the current context.

TO FILL IN A TEXT BOX

- ◆ If the contents of the text box are selected (highlighted), you can replace the entire selection by typing in new text or a number.

- ◆ To edit (change) the contents, press the Home, End, or an arrow key, or click the mouse within the existing text to position the insertion point. *Then* type your changes.

- ◆ To delete text in the dialog box, press the Delete or Backspace key.

- ◆ To select text within a text box, drag the mouse pointer through the text, or double-click the text, or hold down the shift key and use the arrow keys to extend the highlighter through the text you want to select.

- ◆ If the text box contains a number, and has a small up and down arrow to the right of it (see the Granularity option in the above example), you can click the up or down arrows to increase or decrease the number.

TO USE A SCROLL BAR

- ◆ Drag the scroll box, or press the PgUp or PgDn keys, to scroll through all the information in a list or document. Or click the scroll arrows, or press the ↑ or ↓ keys, to move by smaller increments.

NOTE Scroll bars let you view items outside the borders of a list box, or let you set a "sliding scale" option (as for the Scroll Blink Rate in the above example).

TO SELECT A SINGLE ITEM FROM A LIST BOX

- ◆ Click the option you want. Or use the ↑ and ↓ keys to move the highlighter to the option.

Shortcuts: Type the first letter of the item to quickly scroll to the item you want to select. To both select an item and choose the default command button, double-click the item.

NOTE If a list box is too large to fit in the dialog box, it will initially be closed and indicated by an underlined drop-down arrow button (this is called a "drop-down" list). Click the arrow button or press Alt+↓ to open the list.

Some list boxes allow you to select more than one item at a time, as described below.

TO SELECT MULTIPLE SEQUENTIAL ITEMS FROM A LIST BOX

- ◆ Click the first item you want to select, then press and hold the Shift key while clicking the last item.
- ◆ Or use the ↑ or ↓ key to highlight the first item, then press and hold the Shift key while continuing to press the ↑ or ↓ key to select the remaining items. Then release the Shift key.

To cancel your selections, release the Shift key, then click any item in the list or press the ↑ or ↓ key.

TO SELECT MULTIPLE NON-SEQUENTIAL ITEMS IN A LIST BOX

- ◆ Press and hold the Ctrl key while clicking each item you want to select. Release the Ctrl key after selecting the last item.

To cancel a selection, hold down the Ctrl key while clicking the item again, then release the Ctrl key. To cancel all the selections, release the Ctrl key; then click any item in the list, or press the ↑ or ↓ key.

TO SELECT OR DESELECT A CHECK BOX OPTION

◆ Click the option. Or move to the option you want, then press the Spacebar.

NOTE Check boxes let you choose from a list of options that you can switch on and off. When the check box contains an X, the option is selected (or "on"). When the check box is empty, the option is deselected (or "off").

TO USE OPTION BUTTONS

◆ Click the option button you want. Or move the highlighter to one of the buttons in a group, then use the arrow keys to select the option you want. The selected option button will contain a black dot.

NOTE Option buttons (also called "radio buttons") present a number of mutually exclusive options. You can choose only one option button in a group.

TO CHOOSE COMMAND BUTTONS

◆ Click the button you want. Or move to the button you want, then press the Spacebar or ↵. The action you selected will take place immediately.

Shortcut: If the command button is marked with a dark border, simply press ↵ to choose it.

NOTE Some command buttons include special markings in addition to the command name: ... opens another dialog box or lets you provide more information; >> expands the dialog box to show some new options.

Most dialog boxes include these buttons: OK (saves all changes you've made in the dialog box and closes the dialog box); Cancel (closes the dialog box without saving your changes); Help (provides help for the options in the dialog box, then returns to the dialog box).

OK is usually the default button. Pressing Escape (Esc) also chooses the Cancel button.

TO MOVE A DIALOG BOX

- Drag its title bar. Or choose Move from the Control menu for the dialog box, use the arrow keys to move it, then press ↵.

NOTE You can move a dialog box only if it has a title bar or Control-menu box.

TO COMPLETE (OR CANCEL) A DIALOG BOX

- Choose the OK button to close the dialog box and activate your selections. Or choose the Cancel button (or press Esc) to close the dialog box *without* activating or saving your selections.

See Also Control Menu, Help, Menus

DOS APPLICATIONS

You can run a DOS application from Windows using any of the same techniques you use for running Windows applications; by double-clicking the DOS application's icon in Program Manager (if available), or by using **File ➤ Run**, or by double-clicking the application's file name in File Manager. If no PIF file is available for the DOS application, Windows uses the settings in _default.pif.

If you're using Windows in 386 enhanced mode, you can switch between windowed and full-screen size in a DOS application by pressing Alt+↵. To cycle through running applications, press Alt+Tab.

TO COPY TEXT FROM A DOS APPLICATION TO THE CLIPBOARD

1. If the DOS application is in full screen, press Alt+↵ to switch to windowed view.
2. Open the Control menu (press Alt+Spacebar), and choose **Edit ➤ Mark**.

3. Select the text you want to copy by dragging the mouse pointer through it (you can drag the mouse pointer off the edge of the window to scroll additional text into the selection area, if necessary). Release the mouse button when all the text you want is selected.

4. Press ↵ (or open the Control menu again and choose **Edit ➤ Copy**).

A copy of the selected text is now in the Clipboard. You can switch to any other application and choose **Edit➤ Paste** to paste in that text.

TO EXIT A DOS APPLICATION

◆ If you're in Windowed mode, switch to full screen (Alt+↵). Then use the current DOS application's normal procedure to exit the application (e.g. /qy in 1-2-3, the F7 key in WordPerfect.)

DRAG AND DROP

You can perform a number of tasks in Windows by dragging file icons in File Manager and dropping them onto an application or group window, or onto File Manager drive and directory icons.

NOTE Not all applications support drag and drop.

TO DRAG AND DROP

In File Manager, you can perform these tasks by dragging file names:

TO DO THIS	DRAG THE FILE ICON ONTO
Print a file on the default printer	Print Manager window or icon
Create icons in a Program Manager group window	Program Manager group window or icon

TO DO THIS	DRAG THE FILE ICON ONTO
Move or copy files to a different drive or directory	File Manager directory window or directory icon
Move or copy files to a different drive	File Manager drive icon
Open a file in an application	The application's icon or title bar
Embed files as a package	The application's window
Link files as a package	The application's window (press and hold Ctrl+Alt+ Shift while dragging)

If you're using drag-and-drop to move or copy files in File Manager, Windows will automatically either move the file, if you drag to a different directory on the same drive, or copy it, if you drag to a different drive. A plus sign (+) appears in the icon to indicate that you are copying. You can override the default assumptions. Holding down the Ctrl key forces Windows to copy the file; holding down Alt forces Windows to move the file.

When you're using drag-and-drop for other operations, and you're dragging a document file, that file needs to be associated with an application. For example, if you drag a file with the extension .wri to Print Manager, that file will be printed only if the .wri extension is associated with some application. You can use File Manager to associate file name extensions with applications.

See Also Applications, File Manager, Icons, Object Linking and Embedding, Object Packager

DRIVES, DIRECTORIES, AND FILES

All the information stored on your computer, be it applications or documents, is saved in *files*. Files are stored on hard or floppy disks contained in disk *drives*. Each drive has a letter name followed by a colon (:). Typically A: and B: refer to the floppy disk drives, and C:, D:, and higher letters refer to hard disk drives, tape drives, or CD-ROM devices.

To make it easier to work with files, the DOS operating system that Windows uses lets you organize files into a hierarchical structure that can have many levels, much like a company's organization chart or an upside-down tree. This structure consists of *directories* (or *subdirectories*, which are essentially the same as directories, but typically refer to directories below a given directory) and files. The topmost directory on each disk, called the *root*, is automatically created whenever you format a disk. All other directories appear below the root, and each directory can contain its own set of files.

The root directory is named \. Directories below the root can have a name of one to eight characters. No blank spaces are allowed in directory names, nor are any of the following characters permitted:

" / \ [ ] ; : * < > | + = , ?

You use File Manager (or the DOS command MD or MKDIR) to create directories. An application's installation program may also create directories for you automatically.

File names consist of a *base name*, followed by an *extension*. The base name, like a directory name, can be up to eight characters in length. The optional extension always starts with a period (.) and can be up to three characters in length. Neither the base name nor the extension can include blanks or any of the punctuation characters listed above.

Many extensions have special meanings to Windows, including the extensions listed below. (You can also use File Manager to associate other extensions with Windows applications.)

EXTENSION	MEANING
.BAT	Batch file of DOS commands
.BMP	Bitmap file
.CAL	Calendar file
.CHK	Chkdsk command file
.CLP	Clipboard file
.COM	Program file
.CRD	Cardfile file
.EXE	Program file

EXTENSION	MEANING
.GRP	Group file
.MSP	Microsoft paint file
.PAL	Paintbrush color file
.PCX	Paintbrush file
.PIF	Program information file
.REC	Recorder file
.TRM	Terminal file
.TXT	Notepad file
.WAV	Sound file
.WRI	Write file

The following names are reserved and cannot be used for files or directories: CON, AUX, COM1, COM2, COM3, COM4, LPT1, LPT2, LPT3, PRN, and NUL.

In order to open or save a file, the computer must know what *path* to follow. A complete path to a file consists of the drive, followed by each directory (in order from top to bottom), and finally, the file name. Each directory is separated from the next directory below it, and from the file name, by a backslash (\ ) character. Again, no blanks are allowed. For example, the path

c:\windows\msapps\msdraw\msdraw.exe

means "On drive C:, start at the root, then go to the WINDOWS directory, then down to the MSAPPS directory below WINDOWS, then down to the MSDRAW directory below MSAPPS to find the file named MSDRAW.EXE."

When you use the Open or Save As options from an application's File menu, the application typically opens a dialog box that lets you specify a drive, directory, and filename. (The File ➤ Save option is the same as File ➤ Save As when you save a file for the first time.) For example, when you choose **File ➤ Open** from the Write application, you'll see a dialog box like this:

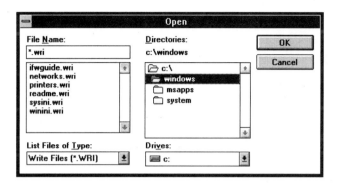

The Save As dialog box is nearly identical, except for its title bar. The parts of the dialog box shown in the above example are as follows:

File Name text box: Shows the currently selected filename. Initially, this box is blank, or it displays a filename or wildcard expression that controls the filenames shown in the File Name list. In this example, ***.wri** means all files in the current drive and directory that have a .WRI extension. The asterisk (*) is a wildcard that stands for any series of characters. If you want to use a different wildcard expression, type the expression you want (e.g., ***.ini** or **test*.doc**), then press ↵.

File Name list: Appears below the File Name text box and lists existing files in the current drive and directory that match the name or wildcard expression shown in the File Name text box.

List Files of Type drop-down list box: Lets you select an extension to replace the one currently in the File Name text box. If you select a different extension from this list box, the File Name list will reflect the filenames in the current directory that match the new wildcard expression.

Directories list: Displays a graphical representation of the directories above the current directory (starting from the root), the current directory, and the subdirectories of the current directory. The current directory is highlighted and also shown below the Directories option name (in this example, the current directory is c:\windows). To switch to a different directory, simply double-click the icon of the directory you want. Again, the File Name list will reflect filenames in the directory you chose.

Drives drop-down list box: Lets you select a different drive. If you select a different drive, the File Name and Directories lists will be adjusted accordingly.

TO SPECIFY A FILENAME
IN THE OPEN OR SAVE AS DIALOG BOX

- ◆ Double-click the filename if it appears in the File Name list, then choose OK.

- ◆ If necessary, in the File Name text box, type the complete path of the file you want to open or save, then choose OK.

- ◆ Or, if the drive and directory icons in the Directories list already indicate that you're at the drive and directory you want, type just the base name (and extension, if necessary) for the file. Then choose OK.

- ◆ Or, open the Drives drop-down list box and select a drive. Then, in the Directories list, double-click the icon of the directory you want. Type the file name in the File Name text box and choose OK.

NOTE Methods for specifying filenames may differ from those given above, depending on the application you're using. For instance, many applications use the Windows 3.0 style dialog boxes, as in the example below. In these dialog boxes you need to scroll to, then double-click the [..] symbol to move up a directory level. Or double-click any directory name, also enclosed in brackets, to move down to that directory. Or, double-click any drive name (e.g. [a], [b], [c]) to switch to that drive.

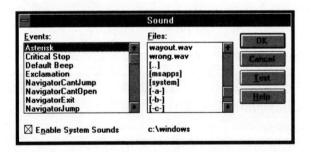

The File Name list may be dimmed when you're saving a file to prevent you from double-clicking a filename and accidentally overwriting it with information from the current document.

See the File Manager entry for information on moving, copying, and renaming files.

See Also Dialog Boxes, File Manager

FILE MANAGER

Windows File Manager helps you organize files and directories, move and copy files, start applications, connect to networks, print documents, maintain disks, and associate a file with an application. When you use File Manager, you work with directory windows, which graphically display the directory structure of your disk, along with the files and directories on the disk.

The following sections explain how to use File Manager to manage, associate, and print files.

TO START FILE MANAGER

Double-click the File Manager icon in the Main group of Program Manager. To start File Manager when you first start Windows, type **win winfile** and press ↵ at the DOS command prompt.

EXAMPLE Here's the File Manager as it initially appears, with a split directory window.

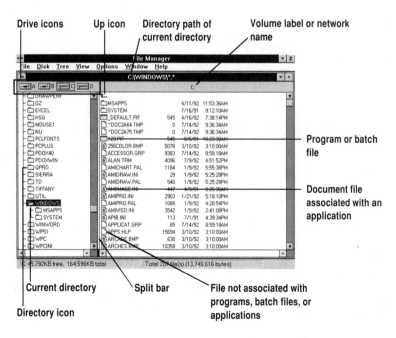

NOTE   The directory window includes these components:

Drive icons: Represent the drives on your computer. Click a drive icon to switch to that drive and replace the current window contents with the contents of the drive you selected. Double-click the icon to switch to that drive and display its contents in a *new* window. (Choose **Window ➤ Tile** or **Window ➤ Cascade** to arrange multiple windows.)

Directory icon: Represents a directory on your disk. Click a directory icon in the directory tree to show that directory's contents. Double-click a directory icon to switch to that directory and show its contents. Double-clicking a directory icon in the directory tree expands the branch; double-clicking the icon again collapses the branch.

Current directory: Indicates the current directory with an open file-folder icon and is highlighted. The current directory's files and subdirectories appear in the right side of the directory window.

File icons: Appear next to file names. The appearance of the icon indicates the file type (see Example). Double-clicking a program or batch file icon runs that program or batch file; double-clicking a file icon that's *associated* with a program starts the application and opens the selected file.

Up icon: The Up icon, shaped like an arrow (↑), takes you up one level in the directory tree when you double-click it.

Split bar: Divides the left and right windows. Drag the split bar to the left or right to narrow or widen the windows.

TO SELECT A FILE OR DIRECTORY

◆   Click on the file or directory icon you want to select.

Shortcut: To select all the files in a directory, click in the right side of the directory window, then press Ctrl+/ (slash).

TO SELECT GROUPS OF ITEMS USING SELECT FILES

1.   Choose **File ➤ Select Files**. You'll see the Select Files dialog box.

2. Type the wildcard expression for files you want to select into the File(s) text box. For example, type ***.txt** for all files with a .TXT extension.

3. To select the group of files, choose the Select button. To deselect (cancel) that group of files, choose the Deselect button.

4. Repeat Step 2 for each group of files you want to select or deselect.

5. Choose the Close button.

TO CHANGE THE VIEW IN THE DIRECTORY WINDOW

Open the View menu. Then choose **Tree and Directory**, **Tree Only**, or **Directory Only**. (The default view is Tree and Directory).

TO CHANGE THE INFORMATION DISPLAYED IN A DIRECTORY WINDOW

Open the View menu, then choose one of these options:

- **Name** to display only the names of files and directories.

- **All File Details** to display file name, size, last modification date and time, and file attributes.

- **Partial Details** to open a dialog box that lets you select which information to display. Choose OK after selecting the options.

TO SORT THE CONTENTS OF A DIRECTORY

Open the View menu, then choose one of these options:

- **Sort By Name** to sort alphabetically by names. Directories appear before files.

- **Sort By Type** to sort alphabetically by extension (e.g., .EXE comes before .INI). Directories appear before files.

- **Sort By Size** to sort by size (largest to smallest). Directories appear before files.

- **Sort By Date** to sort by last modification date (most recent to least recent). Directories appear before files.

TO SPECIFY WHICH TYPES OF FILES ARE DISPLAYED

- Choose **View ➤ By File Type**. Check the types of files you want to display, then choose OK.

NOTE If you choose to display hidden and system files, be careful not to move, delete, or rename them.

TO CREATE A DIRECTORY

1. In the directory tree, select the directory where you want the new directory to appear. (The new directory will be created below the selected directory.)
2. Choose **File ➤ Create Directory**.
3. Type a name for the new directory.
4. Choose OK.

TO SEARCH FOR A FILE OR DIRECTORY

1. In the directory tree, select the directory where you want to start the search.
2. Choose **File ➤ Search**.
3. In the Search For box, type the name or wildcard of the file or directory you want to find.

NOTE The results will appear in a new Search Results window. You can then operate on the files and directories in that window.

TO MOVE AND COPY FILES AND DIRECTORIES USING THE MOUSE

1. Make sure the source and destination windows are visible.

2. Select the source file(s) or source directory. Then do one of the following:

   ◆ To *move* the selected icon(s), hold down the Alt (or Shift) key while dragging the source icon(s) to the destination.

   ◆ To *copy* the selected icon(s), hold down the Ctrl key while dragging the source icon(s) to the destination.

3. Release the mouse button, then release Shift or Ctrl.

4. Choose Yes when prompted to confirm the move or copy.

5. If the destination directory contains a file with the same name as the file you're moving or copying, you'll be asked whether to replace the file. If you're sure you want to replace the file, choose Yes; or choose Yes To All if you're moving or copying multiple files and want to replace all the existing files without being prompted further. Or choose No if you don't want to replace this file.

NOTE The destination can be a directory window, directory icon, or drive icon. If the destination is a drive icon, the moved or copied file(s) are placed in the current directory of that drive. The moved or copied files will have the same names as the original files.

You can also choose **File ➤ Move** or **File ➤ Copy** to move or copy files. These options let you change the names of the destination files, and are similar to the **File ➤ Rename** option described below (see your Windows documentation or File Manager's Help menu for details).

TO DELETE A FILE OR DIRECTORY

1. Select the file(s) or directory you want to delete.

2. Press the Del key.

3. Choose OK from the Delete dialog box that appears. You'll be prompted to confirm the deletion.

4. If you're sure you want to delete the selected file(s) or directory, choose Yes; or choose Yes To All if you're deleting multiple files and want to delete all the selected files without being prompted further. Or choose No if you don't want to delete this file or directory.

NOTE Deleting a directory deletes all files and subdirectories in the directory. Unless you're running MS-DOS 5.0 or higher, or have a file-recovery program, you cannot recover files or directories that you delete accidentally.

TO RENAME A FILE OR DIRECTORY

1. Select the file(s) or directory you want to rename.

2. Choose **File ➤ Rename**.

3. The name of the selected file(s) or directory appears in the From text box. To rename a different file, type the name in the From box.

4. In the To box, type the new name (one that does not already exist in the destination directory). You can specify only one filename in the To box; however, you can use a wildcard (e.g., ***.txt**) to rename a group of files.

5. Choose OK.

TO ASSOCIATE FILES WITH AN APPLICATION

Associating document filename extensions with an application offers several shortcuts for loading, printing, linking, and embedding those documents. For example, if you associate the extension .DOC with Word for Windows, you can double-click any file with that extension in File Manager to load that document directly into Word. You could also print any .DOC file by dragging it to the Print Manager icon.

Take the following steps to associate a document filename extension with an application:

1. Select any file that has the extension you want to associate with an application.

2. Choose **File ➤ Associate**. You'll see the Associate dialog box.

3. The extension you selected appears in the Files With Extension dialog box. You can change this if you wish.

4. In the Associate With box, do one of the following:

   ◆ Select the description of the application you want to associate with this filename extension.

   ◆ Type the complete path name of a program file (e.g., C:\WP51\WP.EXE), or use the Browse button to find the application you want to associate.

   ◆ Choose (None) to remove any association between the extension and an application.

5. Choose OK.

EXAMPLE Here's the Associate dialog box for associating .WP files with Wordperfect for Windows.

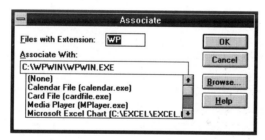

NOTE Applications have a .PIF, .COM, .EXE, or .BAT extension. When a file is associated with an application, a document icon appears next to the filename.

TO PRINT FILES

1. Select the file you want to print.

2. Choose **File ➤ Print**.

3. Choose OK.

NOTE To print this way, the filename extension must be associated with an application, and the application must support printing through File Manager.

See Also Lesson 8, Applications; Dialog Boxes, Drag and Drop; Drives, Directories, and Files

FONTS

A *font* (or typeface) is a collection of letters, numerals, symbols, and punctuation with common characteristics of size and style. After you install Windows, the following types of fonts are available:

- Screen fonts (used to display information on the screen)
- Plotter fonts (used for plotters and some dot-matrix printers)
- TrueType fonts (scalable to any size, these appear exactly the same on-screen as they do when printed; see *TrueType*).

Printers also include built-in fonts, called *printer fonts*, which become available after you install a printer (see *Printers*). You can also use soft fonts and cartridge fonts (see your manufacturer's instructions for installing these).

You can purchase additional fonts for your system. After adding the fonts as described below, you can select them from the Font dialog box or list in your Windows applications.

If the manufacturer provides an installation program and instructions for installing fonts, use those instructions instead of the procedures given here.

TO OPEN THE FONTS DIALOG BOX IN CONTROL PANEL

- Double-click Control Panel in the Main group of Program Manager, then double-click the Fonts icon.

TO ADD SCREEN AND TRUETYPE FONTS

1. Choose the Add button from the Fonts dialog box. You'll see the Add Fonts dialog box.

2. If your fonts are stored on a floppy disk, insert the disk into the drive.

3. Open the Drives list and select the drive containing the new fonts.

4. In the Directories list, select the directory containing the fonts you want to add. The fonts will appear in the List of Fonts box.

5. Select the font or fonts you want to add, or choose the Select All button to select all the fonts from the list.

6. If your fonts are located on a network drive or external drive, and you have sufficient space to store those fonts on your own local hard disk, keep the Copy Fonts to Windows Directory box checked. On the other hand, if the fonts are already stored on your local hard disk, or if you're low on disk space, you can deselect this option. Windows won't copy the fonts to the system directory but, instead, will load them to the current directory.

7. Choose OK to add the font(s).

8. Choose Close from the Fonts dialog box.

EXAMPLE Here's the Add Fonts dialog box with a font selected.

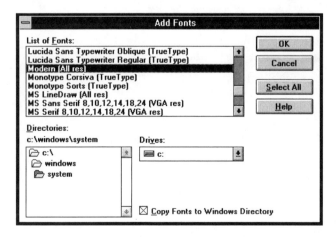

TO REMOVE SCREEN OR TRUETYPE FONTS

1. Select the font (or fonts) you want to remove from the Installed Fonts list in the Fonts dialog box.

2. Choose the Remove button. You'll see the Remove Font dialog box.

3. To remove the selected font(s) from your hard disk (as well as from memory), check the Delete Font File From Disk box. See the Note below for cautions.

4. Choose the Yes button or, if you're removing several fonts and don't want to be prompted to remove each one, choose the Yes To All button.

5. Choose the Close button from the Fonts dialog box.

EXAMPLE Here's the Remove Font dialog box.

NOTE Removing fonts frees up computer memory. If you also want to free up hard disk space, you can check the Delete Font File From Disk box. But be careful not to delete your original font files, or you won't be able to restore the fonts if you decide to use them later. Do not delete the MS Sans Serif font set; if you do, dialog boxes will be difficult to read.

See Also Dialog Boxes, DOS Applications, Printers, TrueType

HELP

The Help system provides a quick way to find more information about any task or command you want to perform, and it is available in most Windows applications.

TO START HELP

- ◆ Choose **Help** from the menu bar, then choose a Help category (see below). Or press F1, then choose a topic from the Help Contents for the application.

- ◆ Or choose the Help button (if it's available) or press F1 in a dialog box to display information about options in that dialog box.

- ◆ Or use the keyboard to highlight an option on the application menus, then press F1 to get help for that option.

Many of these *categories* are available on the Help menu:

COMMAND	DESCRIPTION
Contents (or Index)	Provides an alphabetic list of all Help topics for the application
Search for Help On	Provides a dialog box for locating information about a specific topic (see below).
How to Use Help (or Using Help)	Explains how to use Windows Help. Choose this option if you've never used Help before.
About	Provides information about the application and the environment it's running in.

H

EXAMPLE Here's a Help window from WordPerfect for Windows, with menu options, buttons, and underlined and broken underlined topics.

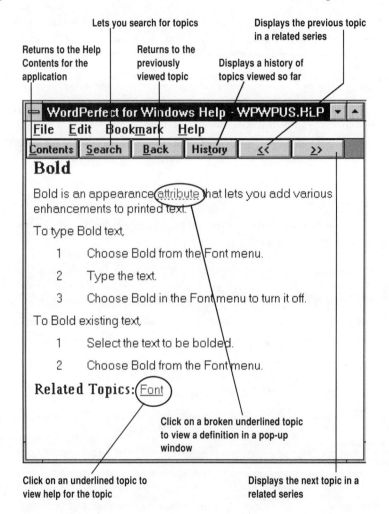

NOTE Help windows include menus (File, Edit, Bookmark, and Help) and buttons. Many also include underlined phrases indicating related topics that you can view, and broken underlining to indicate glossary definitions that you can display.

Not all methods for starting Help are available in all applications, and some applications offer additional options (or differently named options) on the Help menu. For example, Glossary provides a glossary of terms; Keyboard lists keyboard shortcuts; Tutorial provides a tutorial for the application.

The following sections explain tasks you can perform after opening a Help window.

TO USE HELP BUTTONS

Click on the button, or hold down the Alt key while pressing the underlined letter or character that appears on the button. You'll encounter some or all of these buttons:

BUTTON	DESCRIPTION
Contents	Returns you to the Help Contents for your application.
Search	Lets you locate information about a specific topic (see below).
Back	Returns you to the previously viewed topic. You can choose this button repeatedly to retrace your steps through the Help topics.
History	Displays a complete, sequential list of every topic you've viewed during the current session. Choose a topic from the list to review the topic.
Glossary	Displays an alphabetic listing of terms used in the application in a separate window. Choose a term as described under "To display a glossary definition" below. To close the Glossary window, double-click its Control-menu bar, or press Alt+F4.
<<	Displays the previous topic in a series of related topics (dimmed and unavailable when you're at the first topic in the series). Not available in all applications.

BUTTON	DESCRIPTION
>>	Displays the next topic in a series of related topics (dimmed and unavailable when you're at the last topic in the series). Not available in all applications.

TO SEARCH FOR TOPICS

1. Choose the Search button.

2. Select the word or phrase you want to search for, then choose the Show Topics button (or double-click the word or phrase). A list of topics appears at the bottom of the dialog box.

3. Select the topic you want, then choose the Go To button (or double-click the topic).

Shortcuts: To quickly move the highlighter to a word or phrase in Step 2, you can begin typing the first several letters of the phrase you want to search for.

EXAMPLE This example shows the Search dialog box after double-clicking the topic "applications, starting" in Program Manager Help.

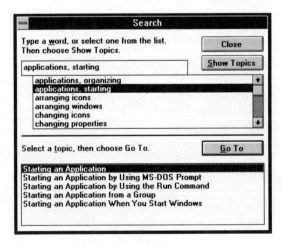

TO CHOOSE A RELATED (UNDERLINED) TOPIC

- Click on the topic you want. Or press Tab until you reach the topic you want, then press ↵.

TO DISPLAY A (BROKEN UNDERLINED) GLOSSARY DEFINITION

- Click on the definition you want. Or press Tab until you reach the definition, then press ↵. The definition appears in a framed, pop-up window. To clear the pop-up window, click the left mouse button, or press Esc, or press ↵.

TO PRINT THE CURRENT HELP TOPIC

Choose **File ➤ Print Topic.**

TO DEFINE A BOOKMARK FOR THE CURRENT TOPIC

1. Choose **Bookmark ➤ Define**. The Bookmark Define dialog box appears (see below).
2. If you want to change the name of the bookmark, type a name in the Bookmark Name text box.
3. Choose OK.

EXAMPLE Here is a sample Bookmark Define dialog box:

```
┌─────────────────────────────────────────┐
│ ─         Bookmark Define                │
│ Bookmark Name:                           │
│ ┌──────────────────────┐   ┌─────────┐   │
│ │Starting an Application│   │   OK    │   │
│ ├──────────────────────┤   └─────────┘   │
│ │Contents              │   ┌─────────┐   │
│ │                      │   │ Cancel  │   │
│ │                      │   └─────────┘   │
│ │                      │   ┌─────────┐   │
│ │                      │   │ Delete  │   │
│ │                      │   └─────────┘   │
│ └──────────────────────┘                 │
└─────────────────────────────────────────┘
```

NOTE Bookmarks let you mark a place in Help before you exit. Then, instead of browsing through Help to return to where you left off, you can simply return to the bookmark.

To delete a bookmark, choose **Bookmark ➤ Define**, select the bookmark you want to delete, choose the Delete button, then choose OK.

TO VIEW AN APPLICATION AND HELP TOGETHER

◆ Choose **Help ➤ Always on Top**.

NOTE This will keep the Help window on top of other windows, so that you can refer to the step-by-step instructions as you use an application.

TO RETURN TO A BOOKMARK

1. Choose **Bookmark** from the menu bar. A numbered list of all the previously defined bookmarks appears.

2. Click the item you want, or press the number that appears next to it.

TO COPY HELP TEXT TO THE CLIPBOARD

1. Choose **Edit ➤ Copy**. The Copy dialog box appears (see below).

2. If you want to copy just part of the topic, select the text you want to copy.

3. Choose the Copy button.

EXAMPLE Here's an example of the Copy dialog box after selecting text and before choosing the Copy button.

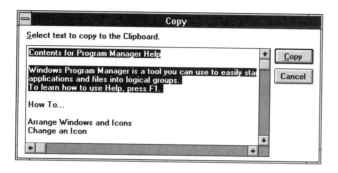

NOTE After copying a topic, you can paste it into a word processing application (choose **Edit ➤ Paste** from the application).

TO ADD COMMENTS (ANNOTATION) TO A HELP WINDOW

1. Choose **Edit ➤ Annotate**. The Annotate text box appears (see below).

2. Type in your own comments, and/or do one of the following:

   ♦ To paste text from the Clipboard into the dialog box at the insertion point, choose the Paste button.

   ♦ To copy text from the dialog box to the Clipboard, select the text and choose the Copy button.

3. Choose the Save button.

EXAMPLE Here's some sample annotation for a Help window.

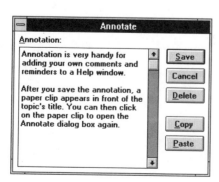

NOTE After you save the annotation, a paper clip appears in front of the topic's title. You can then click on the paper clip to open the Annotate dialog box again.

To remove an annotation, choose **Edit ➤ Annotate** (or click the paper clip), then click the **Delete** button.

TO EXIT HELP

- Double-click the Help window's Control-menu box, or choose **File ➤ Exit**, or press Alt+F4.

See Also Clipboard, Dialog boxes, Menus, Selecting Text and Graphics

ICONS

Icons are small pictures that represent (and give access to) various types of objects (e.g., windows, applications, documents, and files).

TO OPEN AN ICON TO SEE ITS CONTENTS OR RUN THE APPLICATION IT REPRESENTS

- Double-click the icon.

TO REARRANGE ALL ICONS IN THE CURRENT WINDOW

- Choose **Window** ➤ **Arrange Icons** from the Program Manager menu bar. Or choose **Window** ➤ **Cascade** or **Window** ➤ **Tile** to arrange all the open windows and icons.

TO REARRANGE ALL ICONS ON THE DESKTOP

- Call up the Task List (Ctrl+Esc) and choose **Arrange Icons**. Or choose **Cascade** or **Tile** to arrange all the open windows and icons.

TO MOVE AN ICON

- Simply drag the icon to its new location.

I

TO COPY AN APPLICATION
ICON TO A DIFFERENT GROUP WINDOW

- ◆ Hold down the Ctrl key and drag the icon from its current window to another open group window, or to the icon for a closed group window.

TO MOVE AN APPLICATION
ICON TO A DIFFERENT GROUP WINDOW

Drag the icon from its current window to another open group window, or to the icon for a closed group window.

TO DELETE AN ICON

- ◆ Click the icon (once), then choose **File ➤ Delete** from the Program Manager menu bar.

TO CREATE A NEW GROUP WINDOW ICON

1. Starting at Program Manager, choose **File ➤ New**.
2. Choose Program Group, then OK.
3. Type a name for the new group and choose OK.

TO CHANGE AN ICON'S
DESCRIPTION, PICTURE, OR OTHER PROPERTIES

1. Click (once) on the application icon you want to change.
2. Choose **File ➤ Properties** from Program Manager's menu bar.
3. Make whatever changes you wish.

4. Optionally, you can choose Change Icon to change the icon. Icons are available in the files named progman.exe (the default) and moricons.dll (edit the File Name box after choosing Change Icon to see these icons).

5. Choose OK.

NOTE You cannot change the icon for a group window.

TO CREATE AN ICON FOR AN APPLICATION

Install the application as per the manufacturer's instructions, or use Windows ➤ Setup to install an application that's already been copied to your hard disk. Optionally, you can follow these steps to create an icon for a DOS or Windows application:

1. Open (or create) the group window that you want to put the application in.

2. Run File Manager from the Main group, and get to the drive and directory that the application is stored on.

3. Drag the file name for the application into the group window.

TO CREATE AN ICON FOR A DOCUMENT

Perform the same steps as above, but drag a file name for a document that's associated with an application into the group window. For instance, if you drag mycards.crd from c:\windows into a group window, you can run Cardfile with Mycards.crd alrea

dy loaded by double-clicking the new icon that appears.

EXAMPLE On the screen below, we created a group window named Chapters using **File ➤ New**. Then we associated files with the .wp extension to Word-Perfect for Windows, using **File ➤ Associate** in File Manager. To create the icons in the Chapters group window, we dragged the file names for Chap_01.wp,

Chap_02.wp, and so forth from File Manager into the Chapters group window. To open a chapter in the future, we need simply double-click the icon.

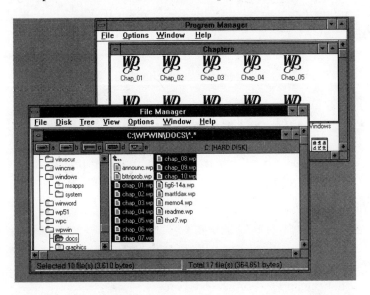

See Also Drag and Drop, Windows

INTERNATIONAL

The International option in Control Panel lets you customize Windows for different languages. Your settings are used by all Windows applications.

TO CHANGE INTERNATIONAL SETTINGS

1. Double-click the Control Panel icon in the Main window of Program Manager, then double-click the International icon.
2. Select the country you want from the Country drop-down list (if it's not already shown in the list box).

3. Select and change any of the other settings.

- To change the Language, Keyboard Layout, or Measurement settings, open the appropriate drop-down list box and select the option you want.

- To change the List Separator setting, move to the List Separator box and type the character that applications should use for separating words or numbers that appear in a series.

- To change the Date Format, Currency Format, Time Format, or Number Format settings, click the appropriate Change button. Then choose options from the next dialog box that appears. Choose OK to return to the International dialog box.

4. Choose OK to return to the Control Panel.

See Also Date/Time, Keyboard

KEYBOARD

The Keyboard option lets you specify how your computer will respond to repeated keystrokes.

TO CUSTOMIZE THE KEYBOARD REPEAT RATE AND DELAY

1. Double-click the Control Panel icon in the Main window of Program Manager, then double-click the Keyboard icon.

2. Drag the scroll box or click the scroll arrows below the Keyboard Speed option you want to change:

- ◆ Use the scroll bar below Delay Before First Repeat to adjust how long it takes the computer to repeat a key after you press and hold it.

- ◆ Use the scroll bar below Repeat Rate to adjust how fast a key repeats when you hold it down.

3. Click in the Test box, then press and hold a letter or number key to test your changes.

4. Choose OK to return to the Control Panel.

NOTE To install a different keyboard driver, use Windows Setup. To choose a different keyboard layout for the currently installed keyboard, use the International option in Control Panel.

See Also International, Windows Setup

MEDIA PLAYER

Media Player lets you operate any Media Control Interface (MCI) multimedia device you've installed, to play either sound (.wav) and MIDI (.mid) files located on your hard disk or program material on the device itself, such as audio CDs. Before you can use any of these devices, however, they must be properly connected to your computer, and any drivers that are required to use the device must be installed as per the manufacturer's instructions.

The buttons on Media Player (shown in Figure 10.6 in the Step-by-Step Tutorial) act just like the buttons on a VCR or tape deck.

TO START MEDIA PLAYER

- ◆ Open the Accessories group window, then double-click Media Player.

TO PLAY A DEVICE

1. If you want to play an audio CD, or some device that does not play directly from files on your hard disk, insert the disk in the player.

2. Choose the Device option on the Media Player menu bar. The devices installed on your computer will be listed.

3. Choose a device from the options shown. If you're *not* playing information stored in a file, skip to step 4.

4. If you're playing a device that requires a file, you'll see an Open file dialog box. Choose the file you want to play.

5. Click the Play button to begin playing.

Once the device starts playing, you can minimize Media Player if you wish, and then continue working with other applications. To stop playing the device, click the Stop button.

NOTE Once Media Player is open and you've selected a device that plays from files, you can use **File ➤ Open** to choose other files to play.

EXITING MEDIA PLAYER

To exit Media Player, choose **File ➤ Exit** or double-click its Control-menu box. If you're playing a device that requires no file, such as an audio CD, the device will continue to play (until you choose the Stop button in Media Player). However, if you're playing a file, the file will stop playing as soon as you exit Media Player.

See Also Lesson 10

MENUS

Windows commands or options are listed on menus. Each application has its own menus, which are listed on the horizontal menu bar just below the title bar of the window.

TO OPEN A MENU

- Click on the name of the menu on the application's menu bar.
- Or press Alt or F10 to highlight the menu bar, then press the ← or → keys to move the menu name you want, and then press ↵.

Shortcuts: Hold down the Alt key while typing the letter that's underlined in the menu name.

NOTE To open the *Control menu* for an application, click the Control-menu box at the upper-left corner of the application's window.

TO SELECT A COMMAND FROM AN OPENED MENU

◆ Click the item you want. Or use the ↑ and ↓ keys to highlight the item you want, then press ⏎.

Shortcut: Type the letter that is underlined in the item name.

TO OPEN A MENU AND CHOOSE A COMMAND

1. Point to any item on the menu bar and hold down the mouse button. A drop-down menu appears.

2. Drag either down to a command or across to choose from another menu.

3. Release the mouse button when you've highlighted the command you want.

NOTE Windows menus use the following conventions:

CONVENTION	MEANING
Dimmed (or invisible) command	The command isn't available at the moment, typically because it doesn't make sense in the current context.
... (ellipsis) after a command	Leads to a dialog box that requests additional information.
✓ (check mark) next to a command	The command is currently in effect. Choose the command again to remove the check mark and turn off the command.
Combination key (e.g., F9 or Ctrl+I)	Indicates a shortcut key for the command. You can press the shortcut key (or key combination) instead of choosing the command from the menus.

219

CONVENTION	MEANING
➤ after the command	Leads to another cascading menu of options.

TO CLOSE A MENU
WITHOUT SELECTING A COMMAND

- Click on a location outside the menu, or press the Esc key.

See Also Control Menu, Dialog Boxes, Windows

MOUSE

The mouse is a pointing device used for many types of operations in Windows.

TO USE THE MOUSE

You should know how to perform the following operations:

OPERATION	METHOD
Point	Position the mouse pointer over a specified item. (The appearance of the mouse pointer depends on the application you're using and the type of operation you're performing at the moment.) You must always point before performing any other mouse operation.

OPERATION	METHOD
Click	Press and release the left mouse button once. You click to select windows, icons, dialog box fields, buttons, check boxes, and graphic objects; and to position the insertion point within text.
Double-click	Press and release the left mouse button twice in quick succession. You double-click to open and expand icons; start applications; choose items from a list; and as a shortcut for selecting (highlighting) a word of text.
Drag	Hold down the left mouse button while you move the mouse. When you're finished, release the left mouse button. You drag to move windows, graphic objects, and icons; to resize windows and graphic objects; and to select (highlight) text and some list items.

NOTE Some applications use the right mouse button to perform special operations.

TO CUSTOMIZE THE MOUSE

1. Double-click the Control Panel icon in the Main window of Program Manager.

2. Double-click the icon for your pointing device in Control Panel (for most users, this is the Mouse icon).

3. Set the options you want, then choose OK.

EXAMPLE Here's the Mouse dialog box for a Microsoft mouse.

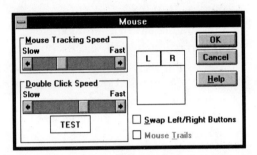

NOTE The options depend on the pointing device you're using. For a Microsoft mouse (or compatible), the options are:

Mouse Tracking Speed: Controls how fast the pointer moves across the screen.

Double Click Speed: Controls how fast Windows registers a double-click of the mouse button. After changing this setting, double-click the Test button in the dialog box to see if you're double-clicking fast enough (the button will change color if you are).

Swap Left/Right Buttons: Switches the functions of the left and right mouse buttons, and may be more convenient if you're left-handed. If you swap the buttons, be sure to click the right (not the left) mouse button to make any further choices.

Mouse Trails: Available only on LCD monitors, this option leaves a trail of pointer icons across the screen.

TO SELECT OR INSTALL
A NEW (OR UPDATED) MOUSE DRIVER

- Choose **Options ➤ Change System Settings** from the Windows Setup menu.

See Also Lesson 3, Control Menu, Dialog Boxes, Icons, Menus, Windows

MS-DOS PROMPT

The MS-DOS Prompt utility lets you run non-Windows applications and DOS commands from the DOS prompt (e.g., C:\>). Be sure to quit MS-DOS Prompt when you're ready to return to Windows and before turning off your computer.

TO START MS-DOS PROMPT

- Double-click MS-DOS Prompt in the Main group of Program Manager.

NOTE Some MS-DOS commands do not work properly with Windows. These include **chkdsk /f, undelete, chcp**, and disk-compaction and optimization programs. You should quit Windows before running these commands.

TO RUN MS-DOS PROMPT IN A WINDOW

- Press Alt+↵. (Press Alt+↵ again to return to a full screen.)

NOTE Alt-↵ is not available when running Windows in standard mode.

TO RETURN TO WINDOWS
WITHOUT QUITTING MS-DOS PROMPT

- ◆ Press Alt+Tab.

TO QUIT MS-DOS PROMPT

- ◆ Type **exit** at the DOS prompt, and press ⏎.

See Also Applications, DOS Applications

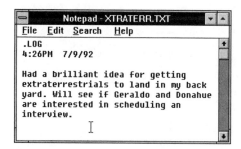

NOTEPAD

Notepad is a simple text editor that's handy for jotting down notes, writing short memos, and creating and editing DOS batch files. Notepad creates and reads files in ASCII text format.

TO START NOTEPAD AND TYPE/EDIT TEXT

- Double-click the Notepad icon in the Accessories group of Program Manager. Within text, use the basic Windows techniques to position the insertion point and edit and select text (Lesson 5).

EXAMPLE Below, we turned on word wrapping, inserted the time and date, and then typed our text. We then moved back to the beginning of the document, typed **.LOG** and pressed ↵ (this causes Notepad to automatically append the time and date to the document each time we open it in the future). Finally, we saved the file with the name xtraterr.txt.

```
┌─────────────────────────────────────┐
│ ▬   Notepad - XTRATERR.TXT    ▼│▲   │
│ File  Edit  Search   Help           │
├─────────────────────────────────────┤
│ .LOG                             ▲  │
│ 4:26PM  7/9/92                      │
│                                     │
│ Had a brilliant idea for getting    │
│ extraterrestrials to land in my back│
│ yard. Will see if Geraldo and Donahue│
│ are interested in scheduling an     │
│ interview.                          │
│                 I                   │
│                                  ▼  │
└─────────────────────────────────────┘
```

NOTE Double-clicking a filename with a .txt extension in File Manager automatically opens Notepad and the document you chose.

TO SET WORD WRAP

- Choose **Edit ➤ Word Wrap**. Choose the option again to turn word wrapping off.

NOTE When editing an ASCII text file, such as a DOS batch (.bat) file, config.sys, or one of the Windows initialization (.ini) files, leave word wrap turned off.

TO ADD THE TIME AND DATE TO A DOCUMENT

- Position the insertion point where you want the time and date to appear, then choose **Edit ➤ Time/Date** (or press F5).

NOTE To create a time-log document that automatically adds the current time and date to the end of the document whenever you open it in Notepad, type **.LOG** (in capital letters) at the left margin of the first line of the document and press ↵.

Notepad uses the system Date and Time, and the International date and time format.

TO SEARCH FOR TEXT IN A NOTEPAD DOCUMENT

1. Move the insertion point to where you want to start the search.
2. Choose **Search ➤ Find**. You'll see the Find dialog box.
3. Type the text you want to find in the Find What box.
4. If you want an exact match of capitalization, select **Match Case**.
5. If you want to change the search direction, select **Up** or **Down**.
6. Choose the Find Next button.

   - If the text was found, it will be selected. You can choose Find Next again, if you wish.
   - If the text wasn't found, you'll see a message. Choose OK to clear the message.

7. Choose Cancel when you're finished searching.

Shortcut: Choose **Find ➤ Next** (or press F3) to bypass the Find dialog box and immediately search for the next occurrence of the same text.

TO MANAGE NOTEPAD DOCUMENTS

Choose these options from the File menu:

OPTION	ACTION TAKEN
New	Opens a new document window. If you haven't saved changes to the current document window, you'll be prompted to do so (choose Yes to save your changes, No to discard them, or Cancel to return to the original document).
Open	Opens an existing document file.
Save	Saves the current document. If this is the first time you've saved a document, you'll be prompted for a filename.
Save As	Saves the current document under a new name.
Print	Prints the current document.
Print Setup	Lets you set various printer options.
Page Setup	Lets you set margins, and adds headers and footers to the current document.

See Also Clipboard; Cut and Paste; Date and Time; Drives, Directories, and Files; International; Selecting Text; Write

OBJECT LINKING AND EMBEDDING

Object Linking and Embedding (OLE) lets you edit objects in one application while working in another. When you *link* an object between its source and destination(s), changes you make in one copy of the object will be reflected in other linked copies. When you *embed* an object, changes you make in one copy are not reflected in any others. A given Windows application can be a client, a server, both a client and a server, or neither (i.e., it doesn't support OLE). To embed an object, you can start either in the source document (server application) or the destination document (client application). To link an object, you start in the source document (server application). See Lesson 7 for more information, and basic OLE terminology.

The general instructions below pertain primarily to the applets that come with Windows (e.g., Write, Cardfile, PaintBrush, and Sound Recorder). Other applications that support OLE may use different procedures, which will be described in their documentation.

NOTE You can only embed or link a *saved* document (one that already has a filename).

TO EMBED OR LINK AN OBJECT (STARTING IN THE SOURCE DOCUMENT)

1. Open the *server* application (e.g., PaintBrush or Sound Recorder).
2. Open the object you're about to link or embed, or create the object and save it to give it a filename.
3. If you're using Sound Recorder, skip this step. Otherwise, select all or part of the object you want to embed or link.
4. Choose **Edit ➤ Copy** to place a copy of the object on the Clipboard.
5. Open the *client* application (e.g., Write or Cardfile).
6. Create or open the destination document.
7. Position the insertion point where you want the embedded or linked object to appear. (In Cardfile, choose **Edit ➤ Picture** instead.)

8. If you want to *embed* the object, choose **Edit ➤ Paste**. If you want to *link* the object, choose **Edit ➤ Paste Link**.

NOTE Starting from the source document (server application) is more flexible than starting from the destination document because it allows you to either embed or link, and it lets you select part of an object (e.g., you can link to just part of a drawing).

If you want to copy an existing link, replace the first three steps above with these:

1. Open the destination document that contains the link you want to copy.

2. If you are using Cardfile, choose **Edit ➤ Picture**.

3. Select the object whose link you want to copy.

TO EMBED AN OBJECT
(STARTING IN THE DESTINATION DOCUMENT)

1. Open the *client* application (e.g., Cardfile or Write).

2. Create or open the destination document where you want to embed the object.

3. Position the insertion point where you want the embedded object to appear. (In Cardfile, choose **Edit ➤ Picture** instead.)

4. Choose **Edit ➤ Insert Object**. You'll see the Insert New Object dialog box.

5. Click the type of object you want to embed (e.g., Paintbrush Picture).

6. What you do next depends on the application you're using:

- If the application's Insert Object dialog box contains a File button, and you want to embed an existing object, click that File button. Then choose the drive, directory, and filename of the object. Choose OK and skip the remaining steps.

- If there is no File button in the Insert Object dialog box, or if you want to create the object at this point, choose OK. Then create the object you want to embed and proceed with the steps below.

WARNING

You cannot use **File ➤ Open** *in the source application to open an existing object at this point, as doing so will break the connection to the destination application. You'll need to start from the source document, as described earlier, to link or embed the existing object.*

7. Choose **File ➤ Update**.

8. Choose **File ➤ Exit & Return To** or **File ➤ Exit** (depending on which Exit option is available).

9. If you're using Sound Recorder, you'll be asked whether to update Sound before proceeding. Choose the Yes button.

EXAMPLE Here's the Insert New Object dialog box before we double-clicked on PaintBrush.

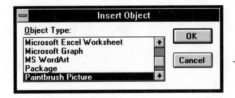

TO EDIT AN EMBEDDED OR LINKED OBJECT

1. If you're using Cardfile, choose **Edit ➤ Picture**.

2. If you're not editing a sound object, simply double-click the embedded or linked object. If you are editing a sound object, select the embedded sound file you want to edit (by clicking on it), then choose **Edit ➤ Sound Object ➤ Edit**.

3. Edit the object as needed.

4. If you're editing an embedded object, choose **File ➤ Update**. If you're editing a linked object, choose **File ➤ Save**.

5. Choose **File ➤ Exit & Return To** or **File ➤ Exit** (depending on which Exit option is available).

TO PLAY AN EMBEDDED OR LINKED SOUND OBJECT

1. If you're using Cardfile, choose **Edit ➤ Picture**.

2. Double-click the object, or click the object to select it, then choose **Edit ➤ Sound Object ➤ Play**.

TO DELETE AN EMBEDDED OR LINKED OBJECT

◆ Select the object and choose **Edit ➤ Cut**.

TO MAINTAIN LINKS

1. Open the destination document that contains the links.

2. If you are using Cardfile, choose **Edit ➤ Picture**.

3. Choose **Edit ➤ Link**. You'll see the Links dialog box.

4. Select the link or links you want to change.

5. Choose the following options or buttons to change the selected link(s):

◆ **Automatic:** Changes the update method to automatic (this is the default).

◆ **Manual:** Changes the update method to manual. With manual selected, the link is updated only when you decide to update it with the Update Now button.

◆ **Update Now:** Updates a manual link.

◆ **Cancel Link:** Breaks a link without removing the object from the document. After breaking a link, you can no longer edit the object from the destination document.

◆ **Change Link:** Lets you link the selected object to a different object. Useful if you accidentally changed the name of the original source document from within the destination document.

◆ **Activate:** If the object is a sound or animation, plays the object. Otherwise, opens the source application for the selected object.

◆ **Edit:** Opens the source application for the selected object.

6. Choose OK to return to the document.

EXAMPLE Here is the Links dialog box for a document containing several links.

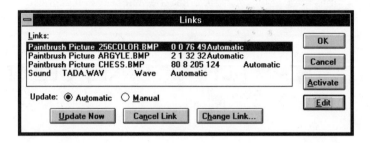

See Also Lesson 9, Cardfile, Cut and Paste, Drag and Drop, Object Packager, PaintBrush, Sound Recorder, Write

OBJECT PACKAGER

Object Packager lets you create a package in the form of an icon. The package can contain a document, such as a spreadsheet, word processing document, picture, or sound; or it can contain another application, such as Calculator or Cardfile, or even an MS-DOS command line. Once you create the package, you can link or embed it into a destination document. Then you'll be able to display the packaged document, or run the application or DOS command, just by double-clicking the icon.

There are four ways of creating a package, one of which uses File Manager instead of Object Packager.

TO CREATE A PACKAGE
USING DRAG AND DROP IN FILE MANAGER

1. Open the destination document in the *client* application and position the insertion point where you want the package to appear. (In Cardfile, choose Edit ➤ Picture.)

2. Switch to Program Manager and double-click File Manager in the Main group.

3. Select the drive and directory containing the documents or applications you want to embed or link.

4. Select the file(s) you want to package. The filename extension of files you embed or link must be *associated* with an application (see File Manager). You can select application or document files (or both).

5. Make sure you can see both the File Manager window and the destination document window. For example, you can press Ctrl+Esc, then choose the Tile button from the Task List.

6. To *embed* the package(s), drag the file icon(s) from the File Manager window to the destination document window. To *link* the package, press Ctrl+Alt+Shift while dragging the icon(s) to the destination window.

NOTE Drag and drop may not be available in all applications. Ctrl+Alt+Shift for linking is erroneously documented in the Windows manual as Ctrl+Shift.

TO OPEN THE OBJECT PACKAGER

◆ Double-click the Object Packager icon in the Accessories window of Program Manager.

EXAMPLE Here we've opened the Object Packager.

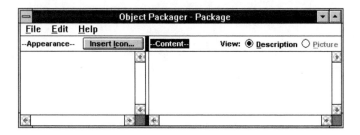

TO PACKAGE AN ENTIRE (EMBEDDED) DOCUMENT

1. Open Object Packager.

2. Click on the Content window.

3. Choose **File ➤ Import**.

4. Select the drive and directory containing the document or application you want to package, then double-click the filename of the document or application you want. The filename extension must be *associated* with an application (see *File Manager*). You can choose an application or a document file.

5. If desired, change the icon or label as described below.

6. Choose **Edit ➤ Copy Package**.

TO PACKAGE ALL OR PART OF A DOCUMENT

1. Open or create the source document that contains the object you want to package or link (you must be using a *server* application such as PaintBrush or Sound Recorder). If you plan to link this object, the document must be named and saved.

2. Select all or part of the object you want to package.

3. Choose **Edit ➤ Copy**.

4. Open the Object Packager.

5. Click on the Content window.

6. If you want to *embed* the package, choose **Edit ➤ Paste**. If you want to *link* the package, choose **Edit ➤ Paste Link**.

7. If desired, change the icon or label as described below.

8. Choose **Edit ➤ Copy Package**.

TO PACKAGE AN MS-DOS COMMAND LINE

1. Open the Object Packager.
2. Choose **Edit ➤ Command Line**.
3. Type the full path of the batch file or program file you want to execute, then choose OK.
4. If desired, change the icon or label as described below.
5. Choose **Edit ➤ Copy Package**.

NOTE You can also use the drag and drop method described previously to package an application or batch file.

TO COPY A PACKAGE TO THE DESTINATION DOCUMENT

1. Open the Object Packager and follow the steps given previously to create a package.
2. Open or switch to the destination document and move the insertion point to where you want the package to appear. (In Cardfile, choose **Edit ➤ Picture**.)
3. Choose **Edit ➤ Paste**.

TO CHANGE THE PACKAGE'S ICON

1. In the Object Packager window, choose the Insert Icon button. You'll see the Insert Icon dialog box.
2. In the Filename text box, type the name of the program file whose icon you want to use (if it doesn't appear already). Or use the Browse button to choose a program file containing the icons you want (progman.exe in the \windows directory contains lots of useful icons).
3. Double-click the icon you want to use.

235

EXAMPLE A sample Insert Icon dialog box appears below:

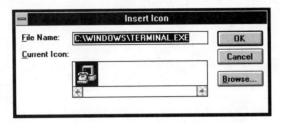

TO CHANGE THE PACKAGE'S LABEL

1. In the Object Packager window, choose **Edit ➤ Label**.
2. Type the new label into the text box.
3. Choose OK.

TO ACTIVATE THE PACKAGE
FROM THE DESTINATION DOCUMENT

♦ In the destination document, double-click the icon for the package you want to display or play. Or choose **Edit ➤ Package Object ➤ Activate Contents**.

TO EDIT AN EXISTING PACKAGE
FROM THE DESTINATION DOCUMENT

1. Open the destination document.
2. Select the icon for the package you want to edit.
3. Choose **Edit ➤ Package Object ➤ Edit Package**. The Object Packager will open.
4. Use Object Packager to make whatever changes are necessary.

5. Choose **File ➤ Update** to update the package.

6. Choose **File ➤ Exit** to quit Object Packager and return to the destination document.

TO DELETE AN EMBEDDED OR LINKED PACKAGE

◆ Select the package and choose **Edit ➤ Cut**.

See Also Lesson 9, Clipboard, Drag and Drop, File Manager, Object Linking and Embedding

PAINTBRUSH

Paintbrush lets you create simple or intricate color drawings. Unlike other Windows accessories, Paintbrush uses both the left and right mouse buttons. You should use the left mouse button unless the right mouse button is explicitly mentioned in the instructions below.

TO START PAINTBRUSH

- ◆ Double-click the Paintbrush icon in the Accessories group of Program Manager.

EXAMPLE The Paintbrush screen appears below in its black and white mode.

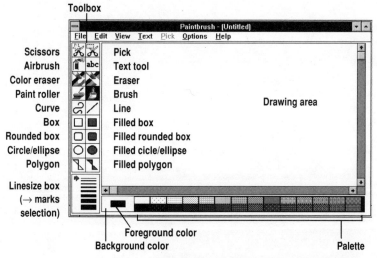

Click left mouse button to select foreground color.
Click right mouse button to select background color.
Double-click left mouse button to customize the color.

NOTE You create your drawings in the *drawing area*. The *cursor* indicates where a line or other object appears when you start drawing, or what you're pointing at when you point outside the drawing area. The size and shape of the cursor in the drawing area depends on the currently selected tool and drawing width.

The *Toolbox* contains the tools you use to create your drawing. To select a tool, click on it in the Toolbox.

The *Palette* displays the colors (in color mode) or patterns (in black and white mode) available for foreground and background areas of your drawing. To select a color or pattern, move the cursor to the color or pattern you want, then:

- ◆ To select the foreground color, click the left mouse button.
- ◆ To select the background color, click the right mouse button.

You can change foreground and background colors at any time.

The *Linesize* box contains the available drawing widths (thickness) of lines made by various drawing tools. To select a drawing width, click on the desired line in the Linesize box. The top line represents a drawing width of one pixel (one pel). The selected drawing width is marked with a $\rightarrow$.

TO CREATE, OPEN, OR SAVE DRAWING FILES

Choose any of the following options from the File menu:

- ◆ **New:** Creates a new drawing file. You can also double-click the Eraser to start a new drawing. (Before creating a new drawing, you can change the background color or pattern for the entire drawing.)
- ◆ **Open:** Opens an existing drawing file.
- ◆ **Save:** Saves your changes to a drawing file (identical to Save As if you're saving a new drawing file).
- ◆ **Save As:** Saves your changes to a drawing file with the name you specify.

TO CHANGE THE DEFAULT DRAWING SIZE
AND CHOOSE BLACK AND WHITE OR COLOR

- Choose **Options ➤ Image Attributes**. Select the desired options (or choose the Default button to return to the default settings). Then choose OK.

NOTE The default settings are based on your display adapter and available memory. You can change width, height, units (inches, centimeters, or pixels), and colors (either black and white or color). Once you've begun a drawing, you cannot change from colors to black and white or vice versa.

TO VIEW THE PICTURE

Choose one of these options from the View menu:

- **View Picture**: (or press Ctrl+P or double-click the Pick tool) Displays a full-screen view of your drawing. Click the mouse anywhere on the screen or press any key to return to the normal display.
- **Zoom Out**: (or press Ctrl+O) Shrinks the drawing to fit into the drawing area. Some drawing options are not available in Zoom Out mode.
- **Zoom In**: (or press Ctrl+N) Returns the drawing to normal resolution size.

TO USE A TOOL IN THE TOOLBOX

1. Select a foreground color or pattern, a background color or pattern, and a drawing width. If you're going to add text, you can also select a font, font size, and font style.
2. Select a tool by clicking on it in the Toolbar.
3. Move the cursor to the drawing area. Then, for most tools, you use the technique of *drag and draw*:
   - Hold down the mouse button and drag the tool in whatever direction you want to draw.
   - When you're finished, release the mouse button.

NOTE Table P.1 summarizes the available tools in order from top to bottom, and left to right.

TABLE P.1: Icon buttons and their associated menu commands

TOOL	DESCRIPTION
Scissors	Defines a free-form cutout area that's outlined with a dotted line. Useful when you want the cutout to closely follow the contours of an object in the drawing. **How to use**: Drag and Draw.
Pick	Defines a rectangular cutout area that's outlined with a dotted line. See "To Use Cutouts." **How to use:** Drag and draw. To view the entire drawing, double-click the Pick tool.
Spray Can	Produces a circular spray of dots in the foreground color or pattern. The drawing width determines the size of the circle of spray. The speed with which you drag the cursor determines the density of the spray. Useful for shading three- dimensional objects. **How to use:** Drag and draw.
Text tool	Adds text at the cursor position in the selected fore ground color or pattern, font, point size, and font style. Text does not automatically wrap from line to line. **How to use:** Choose appropriate options from the Text menu to change font, point size, or font style. Then position the insertion point, click the mouse, then type the text. Press ↵ to start a new line, or reposition the insertion point as needed.
Color Eraser	Changes colors or patterns in all or part of your drawing. The currently selected background color or pattern will replace the selected foreground color or pattern in the drawing. The size of the Color Eraser depends on the drawing width. **How to use:** To change colors or patterns in areas touched by the Color Eraser, use drag and draw. To change every occurrence of one color or pattern to another in whatever part of the drawing is currently visible, double-click the Color Eraser tool in the Toolbox.

P

TABLE P.1: Icon buttons and their associated menu commands (continued)

TOOL	DESCRIPTION
Eraser	If the selected background color or pattern matches the background color or pattern in the area you erase, the Eraser changes all foreground colors or patterns that it touches to the selected background color or pattern. If the background colors or patterns don't match, the Eraser draws with the currently selected background color or pattern. The size of the Eraser depends on the drawing width. **How to use:** Drag and draw. To move the Eraser in a straight horizontal or vertical line, press and hold down the Shift key while dragging. Double-click the Eraser to start a new drawing.
Paint Roller	Fills in any closed shape or area with the selected foreground color or pattern.
How to use:	Click inside the enclosed area that you want to fill with color or pattern.
Brush	Draws freehand shapes and lines in the selected foreground color or pattern and drawing width. **How to use:** Drag and draw. To change the shape of the Brush strokes, double-click the Brush tool in the Toolbox. Then double-click the shape you want.
Curve	Draws curved lines in the selected foreground color or pattern and drawing width.
Line	Draws straight lines in the selected foreground color or pattern and drawing width. **How to use:** Drag and draw. Until you release the left mouse button, you can click the right button to undo the line and start over. To draw a perfectly horizontal, vertical, or 45-degree diagonal line, press and hold down the Shift key while dragging.

TABLE P.1: Icon buttons and their associated menu commands (continued)

TOOL	DESCRIPTION
Box and Filled Box	The Box tool draws hollow rectangles or squares in the selected foreground color or pattern and drawing width. The Filled Box tool draws rectangles or squares that are filled with the selected foreground color or pattern and bordered by the selected background color or pattern. The drawing width determines the thickness of the border. **How to use:** Drag and draw. To draw a perfect hollow or filled *square*, press and hold down the Shift key while dragging.
Rounded Box and Filled Rounded Box	The Rounded Box and Filled Rounded Box tools work the same as the Box and Filled Box tools, except that rounded and filled rounded boxes have round corners. **How to use:** Same as Box and Filled Box.
Circle/ Ellipse and Filled Circle/ Ellipse	The Circle/Ellipse tool draws hollow ellipses or circles in the selected foreground color or pattern and drawing width. The Filled Circle/Ellipse tool draws ellipses or circles that are filled with the selected foreground color or pattern and bordered by the selected background color or pattern. The drawing width determines the thickness of the border. **How to use:** Drag and draw. To draw a perfect hollow or filled *circle*, press and hold down the Shift key while dragging.
Polygon and Filled Polygon	The Polygon tool draws hollow polygons from connected straight-line segments in the selected foreground color or pattern and drawing width. The Filled Polygon tool draws polygons from connected straight-line segments that are filled with the selected foreground color or pattern and bordered by the selected background color or pattern. The drawing width determines the thickness of the border.

P

TO UNDO CHANGES

- Choose **Edit ➤ Undo** or press Ctrl+Z to undo all changes, or press Backspace and then drag the cursor over the parts of the item you want to undo.

TO USE CUTOUTS

After defining a cutout with the Scissors or Pick tool, you can do any of the following:

- To *copy* a cutout to the Clipboard, choose **Edit ➤ Copy** (or press Ctrl+C or Shift+Ins).

- To *cut* a cutout to the Clipboard, choose **Edit ➤ Cut** (or press Ctrl+X or Shift+Del).

- To *paste* a cutout from the Clipboard to the drawing area, choose **Edit ➤ Paste** (or press Ctrl+V or Ctrl+Ins). The cutout appears at the upper-left corner of the drawing.

- To *move* a cutout from one place on the drawing area to another, move the cursor inside the outline and drag the cutout to its new position. You can move transparently or opaquely (see below).

- To *copy* a cutout from one place on the drawing area to another, move the cursor inside the outline, then hold down the Ctrl key while dragging the cutout to its new position. You can copy transparently or opaquely (see below).

- To *sweep* a cutout (leaving a trail of copies behind), move the cursor inside the outline, then hold down the Shift key while dragging the cutout to its new position. The speed with which you drag the mouse determines the density of the trail. You can sweep transparently or opaquely (see below).

- To *anchor* a cutout to its new position, click outside the cutout, or define a new cutout, or select any tool.

NOTE You cannot paste a cutout larger than the current drawing area unless you have zoomed out to display the entire drawing. You can also link, embed, and package cutouts.

TO MOVE, COPY, OR SWEEP TRANSPARENTLY OR OPAQUELY

- Press the *left* mouse button while dragging for a transparent move, copy, or sweep. Or press the *right* mouse button for opaque operations.

NOTE Transparent operations allow your drawing to show through, as long as the background color for the cutout is the same as the currently selected background. Opaque operations (your only option in Zoom Out mode) prevent your drawing from showing through.

TO VIEW THE CURSOR POSITION COORDINATES

- Choose **View ➤ Cursor Position**. The cursor position window appears on the right side of the title bar. You can move it anywhere outside the drawing area.

TO EDIT YOUR CHANGES ONE PEL (PIXEL) AT A TIME

1. Choose **View ➤ Zoom In** or press Ctrl+N.
2. Position the cursor over the area you want to magnify, then click the mouse button. You'll see a magnified version of your drawing, along with a small box in the upper-left to show the area you're editing at normal resolution.
3. Edit the magnified area as follows:

   - Click the *left* mouse button to change a pel to the selected foreground color.
   - Click the *right* mouse button to change a pel to the selected background color.
   - Drag while holding the left or right mouse button to change a wide area of pels to the selected foreground or background color, respectively.
   - Use the Paint Roller to change whole enclosed areas within the magnified area to the selected foreground color or pattern. (Be sure to switch back to the Brush when you're done.)
   - If you make a mistake, choose **Edit ➤ Undo** (or press Ctrl+Z) to undo the changes and return to normal resolution.

4. When you're finished, choose **View ➤ Zoom Out** (or press Ctrl+O) to return to normal resolution.

EXAMPLE Here's a sample button, captured from a screen, where we've zoomed in for detailed editing and cleanup.

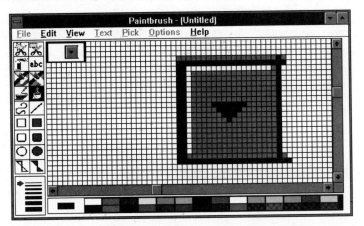

TO PRINT ALL OR PART OF A DRAWING

1. Choose **File ➤ Print**.

2. Choose any of these options:

   - **Quality** (**Proof** or **Draft**): Prints a high-quality drawing using your printer's advanced features (Proof), or an unenhanced drawing using the fastest speed of your printer (Draft).

   - **Window** (**Whole** or **Partial**): Prints the entire window (Whole) or just part of the window (Partial).

   - **Number Of Copies**: Lets you specify how many copies to print.

   - **Scaling**: Lets you specify the scaling for the printed drawing (100% means no scaling).

   - **Use Printer Resolution**: When selected, prints your drawing at printer resolution instead of the screen resolution.

3. Choose OK.

4. If you chose to print a partial window, Paintbrush will display a full-screen version of your drawing. Drag the flexible box to outline the area that you want to print, then release the mouse button.

See Also Lesson 6, Clipboard, Cut and Paste, Object Linking and Embedding, Object Packager, Print Screen

PIF EDITOR

Unlike Windows applications, which are designed to use memory and system resources cooperatively, most DOS applications are designed as though they'll be the only application running at any given time. To make DOS applications act more cooperatively, Windows uses a Program Information File (PIF).

The PIF contains detailed information about a non-Windows application, including the amount of memory the application needs (PIFs are not used for Windows applications). The PIF typically has the same base filename as the associated application's program file, but a .pif extension (e.g., wp.pif is the PIF for WordPerfect's wp.exe program file).

In most cases, you don't need to change a DOS program's PIF settings, because Windows will automatically define the settings for you when you install Windows or use Windows Setup to install the DOS program. It uses predefined PIF settings defined in apps.inf (if any), to take the guesswork out of creating your own PIF settings. If you're a DOS guru, on the other hand, you can change the program's PIF settings to fine-tune the amount of memory and processing resources the program uses.

TO FIND OUT
WHICH PIF AN APPLICATION IS USING

◆ Select the application's icon in the appropriate group window of Program Manager, then choose **File ➤ Properties** (see the Program Manager entry).

NOTE It's possible to define more than one PIF for a given application program, so be sure to determine which PIF is being used by the application whose PIF you want to adjust.

The Command Line text box shows what command is used to start the application. If Windows is using a specific PIF file to run the program, the name of that file appears here. Otherwise, the program's startup command appears with the usual .com, .exe, or .bat extension. In that case, Windows uses the "all-purpose" PIF settings defined in a filenamed _default.pif, on the \windows directory, to run the program.

TO USE THE PIF EDITOR

1. Double-click the PIF Editor icon in the Main group of Program Manager.

2. To edit an existing PIF, choose **File ➤ Open**, and specify the name of the PIF you want. Or, to create a new PIF, choose **File ➤ New**.

3. Choose one of the following modes. The default mode is whichever mode you're running in at the moment.

   - Choose **Mode ➤ 386 Enhanced** to define options that apply when running in 386 enhanced mode.

   - Choose **Mode ➤ Standard** to define options that apply when running in standard mode.

4. Change the PIF options, described below, as required. If you need help determining the appropriate setting for an option, move to that option in the PIF Editor dialog box and press F1 (Help).

5. Choose **File ➤ Save** to save your changes. If prompted, specify a filename that's the same as the base filename of the application (unless another PIF with that name already exists). Then choose OK.

6. Choose **File ➤ Exit**.

PIF SETTINGS FOR 386 ENHANCED MODE If you're designing a PIF file to run a DOS application in 386 Enhanced mode, fill in the prompts as summarized below.

- **Program Filename**: The name of the file that starts the application (typically with a .bat, .com, or .exe extension). If the program's directory is not in the PATH setting of your autoexec.bat file, include drive and directory location (e.g., c:\wp51\wp.exe.).

- **Window Title**: A descriptive name that will appear in the title bar of the application's window. If left blank, the program name without the filename extension will be used.

- **Optional Parameters**: Include any allowable parameters that you want to pass to this application. If you want Windows to prompt you for parameters when you start the program, type a question mark (**?**).

- **Start-up Directory**: Optionally, type the drive and directory that you want to use as the working directory for this application. If you leave this blank, the current directory will be the working directory.

- **Video Memory**: Choose the least amount of video memory required to run the application. Choose Text for programs that don't use graphics (16K), Low Graphics for CGA or Hercules resolution graphics (32K), or High Graphics for EGA and higher resolution (128K). Choosing too low a setting may lead to loss of information on the screen when switching among applications.

- **Memory Requirements**: In KB required, enter the minimum amount of memory that the application requires, as per its documentation. If you're not sure, leave the setting as is. In KB Desired, enter the maximum amount of memory you're willing to allot to the program, up to 640K. You can specify −1 in either or both options to allocate the maximum amount of memory possible.

- **EMS Memory** and **XMS Memory**: These options determine how much *expanded* (EMS) and *extended* (XMS) memory to give this application. In KB Required, enter the minimum amount of memory the application requires, if any, as specified in its documentation. In KB Limit, enter the maximum amount of memory you're willing to allot to the application. A setting of −1 allocates as much memory as the program requests, a setting of 0 prevents the application from using expanded or extended memory.

- **Display Usage**: Choose Full Screen to start this application in full-screen mode. Otherwise choose Windowed to start the application in a window.

P

Regardless of which display mode you choose, you can still press Alt+⏎ to switch between modes while the application is running.

- **Execution**: Choosing Background tells Windows to keep running this application even when its window isn't selected. If you don't select this option, the application is suspended when it's not in the active window. Choosing Exclusive tells Windows to suspend all *other* applications that are in the background while the application is running. The default is neither option; the application runs only when it's in the foreground, and never prevents other applications from running in the background.

- **Close Window on Exit**: If checked, closing this application's window returns you to Windows immediately. Leaving this option unchecked pauses before returning you to Windows, giving you time to read any closing (or error) messages that might appear.

ADVANCED 386 ENHANCED SETTINGS Choosing Advanced from the first PIF Editor screen leads to more advanced options that help you fine-tune memory and resource usage, and troubleshoot specific problems with the screen display.

- **Background Priority**: Specify the amount of CPU resources the program will be given when running in the background, from 0 (none) to 10000 (all). The default setting is 50.

- **Foreground Priority**: Specify the amount of CPU resources the program will be given when running in the foreground, from 0 (none) to 10000 (all). The default setting is 100.

- **Detect Idle Time**: If you choose this option, Windows will pass resources to other applications when the program is idle. Otherwise, the program will be given resources even when it is idle in memory, thereby maximizing its response time at the cost of slowing down other running applications.

- **EMS Memory Locked, XMS Memory Locked**, and **Lock Application Memory**: If any option is checked, that type of memory will not be swapped to disk. Locking memory might improve the performance of the application while it's running, at the cost of slowing down all other running programs.

- **Uses High Memory Area**: If checked, allows the application to use its own high memory area. Clear this option if the program conflicts with memory requirements of other applications or hardware, such as a network card.

- **Monitor Ports**: If the application is not displayed correctly when switching from windowed to full-screen mode, choose the same option here as you chose under Video Mode earlier. But doing so will slow down the application a little, so don't choose any options unless you're having problems.

- **Emulate Text Mode**: If this application runs in Text display mode, and its screen is garbled or the cursor is out of whack, clearing this check box may fix the problem.

- **Retain Video Memory**: Choosing this option tells Windows to monitor the display port to prevent problems when the application switches from one display mode to another. This slows down full-screen screen displays, but may resolve any problems the application has running in full-screen mode.

- **Allow Fast Paste**: If you have problems pasting data into the application, deselect this option to slow down the paste speed.

- **Allow Close When Active**: If you select this option, the application will be closed automatically when you exit Windows. However, choosing this option can lead to data loss and corrupted files. Leaving this option cleared prevents you from leaving Windows until the application is closed.

- **Reserve Shortcut Keys**: If the application uses any of the same shortcut keys that Windows uses, checking the appropriate shortcut key here tells Windows to send that shortcut keypress to this application, rather than to Windows.

- **Application Shortcut Key**: Lets you define your own shortcut key for starting the application from Program Manager, and for switching to its window once it's active. To prevent conflicts with other shortcut keys, use a Ctrl+Shift+*key* combination.

PIF SETTINGS FOR STANDARD MODE If you are designing a PIF for running a DOS application in Standard mode, most of the options will be similar to those described under "PIF Settings for 386 Enhanced Mode" above. Additional options include:

- **Directly Modifies**: Choose any serial port(s) that the application uses (COM1, COM2, COM3, or COM4) to prevent other applications from trying to use the same port while the application is running. If the application has its own keyboard buffer, you may need to select this option to run the application properly. However, if you choose this option you'll need to exit this application when you want to return to Windows—you won't be able to switch to other applications.

- **No Screen Exchange:** Selecting this option conserves a little extra memory for the application, but prevents you from using PrintScreen or Alt+PrintScreen to copy screen shots to the Windows Clipboard.

- **Prevent Program Switch:** If you choose this option you won't be able to switch from this application to others. This conserves a little memory, but requires that you exit the application when you want to return to Windows.

- **No Save Screen:** Tells Windows not to save a copy of the application's screen when you switch to another application, which can conserve some memory. However, when you return to the application, the information on the screen may not be correct.

EXAMPLE Here's a sample PIF for running WordPerfect 5.1 for DOS in 386 enhanced mode.

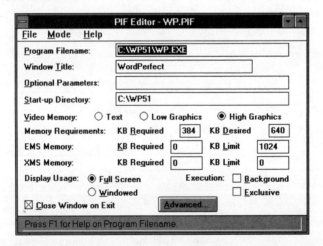

WARNING

Be careful when changing PIF settings because they affect how, and even whether, the application runs. Please see your Windows documentation for detailed information.

See Also 386 Enhanced Mode, Windows Setup

PRINT MANAGER

Print Manager oversees all the printing operations on your Windows system. It works in the background, sending your files to the printer while you continue working. When Print Manager is activated (as it is by default), Windows applications will use it to print files. Non-Windows applications do not use Print Manager.

The information below pertains to local (non-network) printers. Please see your Windows documentation (and network administrator) for details about using Print Manager on a network.

Print Manager also lets you control a printer's setup; see the Printers entry for this option.

TO ACTIVATE PRINT MANAGER

Because Print Manager is normally turned on, you won't need to follow these steps unless you have turned it off.

1. Double-click Control Panel in the Main group of Program Manager, then double-click the Printers icon.
2. Check the Use Print Manager box if it isn't already checked.
3. Choose Close.

TO PRINT A DOCUMENT USING PRINT MANAGER

◆ Choose **File ➤ Print** from the application's menu.

TO OPEN THE PRINT MANAGER WINDOW AND VIEW THE QUEUES

◆ Double-click the Print Manager icon in the Main group of program manager.

EXAMPLE The printer in this example is paused, with three files in the print queue.

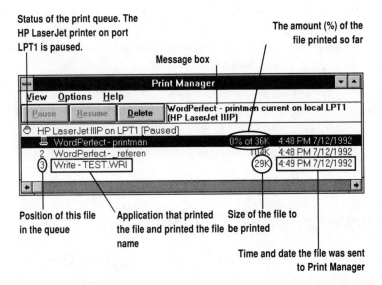

Status of the print queue. The HP LaserJet printer on port LPT1 is paused.

The amount (%) of the file printed so far

Message box

Position of this file in the queue

Application that printed the file and printed the file name

Size of the file to be printed

Time and date the file was sent to Print Manager

TO CHANGE THE ORDER OF THE PRINT QUEUE

♦ Drag the file whose position you want to change to its new position in the Print Manager window.

TO PAUSE OR RESUME PRINTING

1. In the Print Manager window, select the printer or file you want to pause (suspend) or resume.

2. To pause the printing, choose the Pause button. To resume the printing, choose the Resume button.

TO DELETE A FILE FROM THE QUEUE

♦ In the Print Manager window, select the file you want to delete. Choose the Delete button, then choose OK.

TO RESPOND TO A
PRINTING ERROR OR CANCEL A PRINT JOB

If a minor printer error occurs during a print job (for example, if the printer runs out of paper), you'll see an error message with options to Retry or Cancel. Typically, correcting the problem at the printer (e.g., loading paper) and then choosing Retry will fix the problem. If you want to cancel the print job:

1. Choose Cancel from the error message box.
2. Switch to Print Manager (press Ctrl+Esc then double-click Print Manager in the Task List, or just double-click the Print Manager icon at the bottom of the screen if it's visible).
3. Click the name of the file that you don't want to print.
4. Choose Delete.
5. To cancel all pending print jobs, choose **View ➤ Exit**. To resume remaining print jobs, just minimize Print Manager's window.

See Also Fonts, Printers

PRINT SCREEN

You can use the Print Screen key to create a snapshot of an entire screen or window and copy it to the Clipboard.

TO COPY AN ENTIRE SCREEN TO THE CLIPBOARD

1. Set up the screen as you want the printed copy to look.
2. Press PrintScreen (or Shift+PrintScreen if PrintScreen alone doesn't work with your keyboard).

NOTE The copied screen may be in bitmap (.bmp) or text format.

TO COPY THE ACTIVE WINDOW TO THE CLIPBOARD

1. Make sure the window you want to copy is the active window (by clicking on the window).

2. Press Alt+PrintScreen (or Alt+Shift+PrintScreen if Alt+PrintScreen alone doesn't work with your keyboard).

NOTE A non-Windows application must be running in a window in 386 enhanced mode. The copied window is always in bitmap (.BMP) format.

TO PRINT THE CURRENT SCREEN

If you simply want to print the captured screen or window, and don't need to save it or edit it, you can paste it into a Write document, then print it by following these steps:

1. After capturing a screen or window, open the Accessories group, then double-click the Write icon.

2. Choose **Edit ➤ Paste**.

3. Choose **File ➤ Print**, then choose OK.

4. When the print job is done, you can close the Write document without saving the current document.

TO EDIT THE SCREEN AND/OR SAVE IT AS A BITMAP FILE

If you want to edit the captured screen or window (perhaps to isolate a button or menu), and/or want to save the screen as a bitmap file, you can paste the image into Paintbrush. However, to ensure that Paintbrush doesn't crop the image, you may need to jump through a couple of extra hoops:

1. After capturing your screen or window, open the Accessories group, then double-click Paintbrush to open it.

2. Maximize Paintbrush to full screen size.

3. Choose **Options ➤ Image Attributes**.

4. Choose **pels** (pixels), then set the Width and Height to the pixel height and width of your monitor (or 50 or so pixels larger, if you want to have a little border around the image for cutting and pasting.) Common resolutions are 640 x 480 (VGA), 800 x 600 (Super VGA), 1024 x 768 (XGA, TIGA, other Super VGA).

5. Choose Colors or Black and White (whichever you prefer), then choose OK.

6. Choose **File ➤ New** to create a drawing area with your current settings.

7. Choose **View ➤ Zoom Out**.

8. Choose **Edit ➤ Paste** or press Ctrl+V. Initially, the capture appears as a grayish grid.

9. Click any tool in the tool bar, such as the spray can or paint brush. You may hear a beep, then your screen capture appears on the screen.

10. Now zoom back in by choosing **View ➤ Zoom In**.

The image may appear to be cropped, but you can use the scroll bars to verify that the entire screen is in Paintbrush. Now you can edit the screen as you would any other Paintbrush picture, and save it with the usual **File ➤ Save** commands.

To print the image from Paintbrush, choose **File ➤ Print**. For best results, you might want to try selecting the Use Printer Resolution check box in the Print dialog box, then set the Scaling option to 200 or 300%.

NOTE To isolate a button, menu, or other small portion of a captured screen, define the area you want to save as a cutout, then remove the background. To clean up the small saved portion, use **View ➤ Zoom In**. (See Paintbrush for more information).

If you work with captured screens often, consider purchasing a product that's specifically designed to do the job. (We used Collage from Inner Media for screen captures in this book.)

See Also Lesson 6, Applications, Clipboard, Paintbrush

257

PRINTERS

Before you can print in Windows, you need to connect your printer to your computer, then install it. The installation process involves using options in the Printers dialog box to add the appropriate *printer-driver* file, select a printer port (if your printer isn't connected to LPT1), change printer-specific settings (optional), and choose the default printer (if your printer has multiple printers attached). You can also add and remove printer fonts (see *Fonts*).

See the manufacturer's instructions for details on installing printer drivers provided by the device manufacturer and not included with Windows. See the Windows documentation for details on installing laser printers with a PostScript cartridge.

TO ACCESS THE PRINTERS DIALOG
BOX FOR UPDATING PRINTER DRIVERS

1. Connect your printer to your computer according to the manufacturer's instructions.

2. Read the printers.wri Read Me file supplied with Windows, and your manufacturer's documentation to learn about your printer.

3. Wait until any current printing is complete.

4. Double-click Control Panel in the Main group of Program Manager, then double-click the Printers icon. Or, double-click Print Manager in the Main group of Program Manager, then choose **Options ➤ Printer Settings**. You'll see the Printers dialog box.

EXAMPLE The Printers dialog box lets you add, remove, and change settings for printer drivers. In this example, we've chosen the Add~GT~GT button, which opens the List of Printers list.

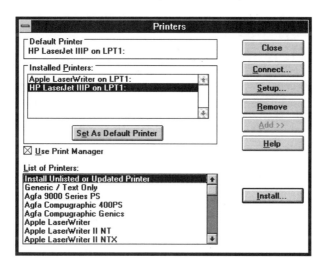

NOTE After opening the Printers dialog box as described above, you can perform any of the following tasks. When you're finished with the Printers dialog box, choose Close.

TO ADD A PRINTER

1. Choose the Add>> button. You'll see the List of Printers list shown above.
2. Select the exact name of the printer you want to install from the List of Printers list.
3. Choose the Install button.
4. When prompted, insert the disk containing the printer driver you want to install into drive A. Or type the drive and directory name (*not* the driver filename) where the driver is located.
5. Choose OK from the Install Driver dialog box.
6. Follow any on-screen instructions that appear.

NOTE If the printer is not connected to LPT1, you need to change the port assignment, as described next.

TO CONNECT THE PRINTER
TO A PORT OTHER THAN LPT1

1. Select the printer whose port assignment you want to change from the Installed Printers list.

2. Choose the Connect button. You'll see the Connect dialog box.

3. Select the port you want to assign the printer to.

4. If you selected a serial port (COM), choose the Settings button, change the settings if necessary, then choose OK.

5. If you want to connect to a network printer, choose the Network button, change the settings as required (see your Network Administrator if you need help), then choose Close.

6. Choose OK to return to the Printers dialog box.

NOTE You can connect printers to the following ports:

PORT	DESCRIPTION
LPT	Parallel port.
COM	Serial port.
EPT	IBM Personal Pageprinter port (requires a special card).
FILE	Prints to a file instead of a printer. Some applications also support printing to files even if you don't select the FILE port.

If you change ports, you should double-check the printer setup options to see that they're still correct.

TO CHANGE PRINTER SETUP OPTIONS

1. Select the printer whose settings you want to change from the Installed Printers list.

2. Choose the Setup button. You'll see the Setup dialog box.

3. Choose the necessary options for your printer (options vary for each printer).

4. Choose OK to return to the Printers dialog box.

EXAMPLE This Setup dialog box is for an HP LaserJet IIIP printer.

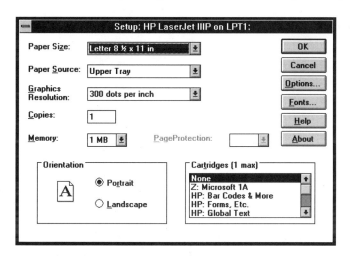

TO CHOOSE A DEFAULT PRINTER

1. Select the printer you want from the Installed Printers list.

2. Choose the Set as Default Printer button.

NOTE Use this option if you have several printers installed and want to change the default printer.

TO REMOVE INSTALLED PRINTER DRIVERS

1. Select the printer you want to remove from the Installed Printers list.

2. Choose the Remove button.

3. When asked to verify the deletion, choose the Yes button.

See Also Fonts, Print Manager

RECORDER

The Recorder applet lets you create *macros*, which are recorded keystrokes and mouse actions that you can play back later simply by pressing a key. Recorder is designed for Windows applications only. You can store many macros in a single recorder file (.rec), and can save as many recorder files as you want. You may wish to group macros for the same application together into a single recorder file.

TO START RECORDER

- Double-click the Recorder icon in the Accessories group of Program Manager.

EXAMPLE Here's the Recorder window for a recorder file containing two macros.

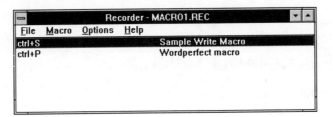

TO RECORD A SIMPLE MACRO

1. Start Recorder.
2. Open or switch to the application for which you want to record the macro, then move the insertion to where you want to start recording.
3. Switch to Recorder and choose **Macro ➤ Record**. You'll see the Record Macro dialog box.
4. In the Record Macro Name box, type a name for the macro.

5. Assign the macro shortcut keystroke as follows:

- In the Shortcut Key box, type the keyboard key you want to use as a shortcut key. Or open the Shortcut Key drop-down list and select a key.
- Check one or more of the Ctrl, Shift, or Alt check boxes.

The checked keys are used in combination with the key assigned in the Shortcut Key box to play back the macro (e.g., Ctrl+S, Ctrl+Alt+Shift+ Space, Ctrl+F2, and so forth).

6. In the Description box, type a detailed description of the macro (optional).

7. Optionally, make selections in the Playback area (although the default settings are usually adequate):

- **To**: Play back to the Same Application from which the macro was recorded, or to Any Application.
- **Speed**: Play back at Fast speed, or at the Recorded Speed (slow).
- **Continuous Loop**: Check the box to play back the macro continuously (useful for demos). Leave it unchecked to play back only once.
- **Enable Shortcut Keys**: Removing the check mark prevents playback with shortcut keys.

8. Choose the Start button to begin recording. Recorder becomes a flashing icon and continues flashing until recording stops.

9. Type the keystrokes and perform the mouse actions you want to record (for best results, avoid using the mouse).

10. To stop recording, press Ctrl+Break.

11. Select Save Macro from the dialog box that appears, then choose OK.

EXAMPLE A completed Record Macro dialog box appears below.

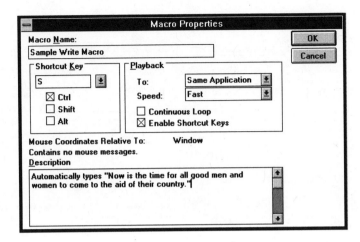

NOTE All the shortcut keys in a given recorder file must be unique, though other recorder files can reuse shortcut keys. Avoid assigning shortcut keystrokes that are also used by your Windows application. When a recorder file is active, its shortcuts will take precedence over the application's shortcuts.

See your Windows documentation or Recorder's Help menu options for details on Record Mouse and Relative To options.

TO SAVE CHANGES TO A MACRO FILE

Choose **File ➤ Save** from the Recorder menu. If prompted, specify a drive, directory, and filename (no extension). Windows will add the .rec extension to whatever file name you provide.

TO OPEN AN EXISTING MACRO FILE

Choose **File ➤ Open** from the Recorder menu and specify a drive, directory, and filename.

TO DELETE A MACRO
FROM AN OPENED MACRO FILE

Select the macro you want to delete, then choose **Macro ➤ Delete**.

TO PLAY BACK A MACRO

1. Position the insertion point in the document where you want the macro to play back.
2. Open the Recorder if it's not already open.
3. Open the recorder file containing the macro you want to play back (if it's not already open).
4. Press the shortcut key you assigned to the macro, or double-click the macro name.

Shortcut: After opening the recorder file containing your macro, you can run any macro in the file as often as you wish by simply positioning the insertion point in your application document and pressing the appropriate shortcut key.

TO STOP A MACRO
WHILE IT IS PLAYING BACK

- Press Ctrl+Break, then choose OK when prompted.

See Also Drives, Directories, and Files

SCREEN COLORS

The Colors option in Control Panel lets you customize the colors of every part of your desktop. You can use a color scheme that comes with Windows, or you can define your own.

TO SELECT A COLOR SCHEME

1. Double-click the Control Panel icon in the Main group of Program Manager, then double-click the Color icon. You'll see the Color dialog box.

2. Open the Color Schemes drop-down list box and select a color scheme from the list. The sample screen in the dialog box will display the current color selections.

3. Choose OK to save your selections and return to Control Panel.

TO ADD, CHANGE, OR REMOVE A COLOR SCHEME

1. Perform Steps 1 and 2 above to choose the color scheme you want to change or remove, or to choose the color scheme to use as the basis for a new one.

2. If you want to remove the selected color scheme, choose the Remove Scheme button, choose Yes to verify the deletion, then choose OK. Skip the remaining steps.

3. Click the Color Palette>> button. The Color dialog box expands (see above example).

4. Select the desired element from the Screen Element list. Or, in the sample screen, click the part of the screen whose color you want to change.

5. In the Basic Colors palette, click the color you want. The sample screen will change accordingly.

6. Repeat Steps 4 and 5 for each area you want to color.

7. Choose Save Scheme to save your changes, type a name for your new scheme in the text box that appears, then choose OK. (You should give your custom setups different names from those supplied with Windows.)

8. Choose OK to save your changes and return to Control Panel.

NOTE When you click areas in the sample screen, the Sample Element list box shows which element is selected at the moment.

SCREEN SAVER

A screen saver is a utility program that displays a moving pattern (or text) while your system is turned on but has been inactive for a specified interval. Pressing a key or moving the mouse clears the screen saver and redisplays the application. The Control Panel offers several screen savers that work while Windows is running.

TO SELECT A SCREEN SAVER

1. Double-click the Control Panel icon in the Main group of Program Manager, then double-click the Desktop icon. You'll see the Desktop dialog box.
2. Open the Name drop-down list box in the Screen Saver area and select a screen saver from the list.
3. In the Delay box, specify the number of minutes of inactivity that should elapse before the screen saver appears.
4. To test the screen saver, click the Test button. To end the test, press a key or click the mouse.
5. Choose OK to save your settings and return to Control Panel.

NOTE To remove the screen saver, select (None) from the top of the Name list.

TO CUSTOMIZE A SCREEN SAVER OR ADD, CHANGE, OR REMOVE A PASSWORD

1. Select the screen saver as described in Steps 1 and 2 above, then choose the Setup button.

267

2. Choose the Setup button.

3. Change any settings you want (these depend on which screen saver is currently selected).

- ◆ To add or change a password, select (check) Password Protected in the Password Options area. Then choose the Set Password button, and complete the appropriate text boxes in the Change Password dialog box that appears. Then choose OK.

- ◆ To remove password protection from a screen saver, remove the check from the Password Protected check box.

4. Choose OK to return to the Desktop dialog box.

NOTE Different screen savers offer different customization options. If you add a password, you must type the password before you can return to Windows from the screen saver.

SELECTING TEXT

Before making changes to blocks of text, you must select the text (selected text appears highlighted on the screen). The selection techniques described here work in most text editing programs and in the text box options of dialog boxes.

TO SELECT TEXT

1. Move the mouse pointer to the first character you want to select.

2. Hold down the left mouse button and drag the insertion point to the last character you want to select.

3. Release the mouse button.

or...

1. Move the insertion point to the first character you want to select (by using insertion point positioning keys or clicking the mouse).

2. Hold down the Shift key while you press insertion point positioning keys to extend the selection to the last character you want to select.

3. Release the keys.

Shortcuts: Some applications let you double-click to select a word, and some let you choose **Edit ➤ Select All** to select all the text in a document.

NOTE See Lesson 5 for a complete list of insertion point positioning keys used in Windows applications.

TO CANCEL A SELECTION

◆ Click anywhere in the document or press an arrow key.

See Also Lesson 5, Dialog Boxes, Write

SELECTING GRAPHICS

To copy a graphic image to the Clipboard in order to paste, link, or embed that image in some other document, you first need to select the graphic. The exact technique you'll use depends on the application you're using, but we can describe some fairly common techniques here.

TO SELECT A GRAPHIC IMAGE

◆ Click the graphic once, or…

◆ If you're using Paintbrush, choose the Scissors or Pick tool and drag a frame around the graphic,

◆ Or, choose **Edit ➤ Select All** (if it's available in the current application.)

If none of these techniques work, check the documentation for the application.

See Also Lesson 6, Cut and Paste, Object Linking and Embedding

SOUND

The Sound icon in Control Panel lets you assign custom sounds to Windows events if you have a sound card and its driver installed.

TO ASSIGN A SOUND TO AN EVENT

1. Open the Main group window, then open Control Panel.

2. Double-click the Sound icon.

3. Click an event (such as Windows Start or Windows Exit) to which you want to assign a sound.

4. Click the name of the sound (.wav file) that you want to assign to that event. (To test the sound, double-click it or click once and choose Test.)

5. Repeat steps 3 and 4 for as many events as you wish.

6. Make sure Enable System Sounds is selected (marked with an X), then choose OK.

EXAMPLE In the Sound dialog box below, we've assigned a sound stored in the file yikes.wav to the appearance of any dialog box that contains an exclamation point icon.

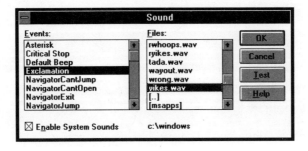

SEE ALSO Lesson 3, Object Linking and Embedding, Object Packager, Sound Recorder

SOUND RECORDER

Sound Recorder lets you play sounds, and also record them if you have installed the appropriate hardware and driver.

TO START SOUND RECORDER

◆ Open the Accessories group, then double-click the Sound Recorder icon. The buttons in Sound Recorder work like those on a VCR or tape deck, as shown below.

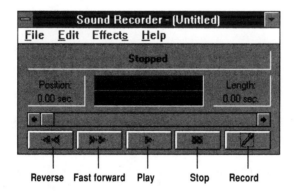

Reverse   Fast forward   Play   Stop   Record

TO OPEN AND PLAY EXISTING SOUND FILE

1. Choose **File ➤ Open** from Sound Recorder's menu bar.
2. Double-click the name of the sound file you want to hear.
3. Click the Play button.

271

TO CHANGE THE SPEED OR VOLUME OF A SOUND, OR ADD SPECIAL EFFECTS

- ◆ Choose an option from the Effects menu, then click the Play button to hear the sound with the effect added. To undo changes to a sound, choose **File ➤ Revert**, then choose **Yes**.

TO EDIT A SOUND

1. Drag the scroll box to the position within the sound file where you want to insert, mix, or delete sound (the Position indicator shows the position of the scroll box as the number of seconds into the sound.) Then…

   - ◆ To insert a new sound, choose **Edit ➤ Insert File**, and choose the sound file you want to insert.
   - ◆ To mix another sound into the current one, **Edit ➤ Mix with File**, then choose the file to mix in.
   - ◆ To delete part of the sound, choose **Edit ➤ Delete Before Current Position**, or **Edit ➤ Delete After Current Position**.

2. To hear the changes, click the Rewind button, then click the Play button.

NOTE As the names imply, when you *mix* a new sound into an existing sound, both sounds are combined into one sound and played back simultaneously. When you *insert* a sound, the new sound is played independently at whatever point you inserted it.

TO RECORD A SOUND

1. Follow the instructions in your sound card's documentation to correctly connect the microphone and adjust its recording volume.
2. Choose **File ➤ New** if you want to start with a clean slate.
3. Click the Record button, and record your sound (up to one minute.)
4. Click the Stop button when done.

5. Click Rewind, then Play, to hear the recorded sound.

6. Choose **File ➤ Save As** to save the sound.

TO COPY THE CURRENT SOUND TO THE CLIPBOARD

- ◆ Choose **Edit ➤ Copy**.

SEE ALSO Lesson 10, Object Linking and Embedding, Object Packager, Sound

TASK LIST

Task List lets you switch among running applications, arrange application windows and icons, and terminate applications.

TO OPEN THE TASK LIST

- Press Ctrl+Esc.
- Or open the Control menu (by clicking the Control-menu box) and choose **Switch To**.
- Or double-click anywhere on the desktop, *outside* any open windows and away from icons.

EXAMPLE This sample Task List shows several running applications.

NOTE You must open the Task List before performing any of the following operations. Choosing a button in the Task List performs the action and automatically closes the Task List. To close the Task List without making a selection, press Esc or choose Cancel.

TO SWITCH TO
AN APPLICATION USING THE TASK LIST

- Double-click the name of the application you want to switch to. Or select the application name, then choose the Switch To button.

TO END A WINDOWS
APPLICATION FROM THE TASK LIST

- Select the name of the application you want to end, then choose the **End Task** button. If the application has any open documents, you'll be prompted to save the changes.

TO ARRANGE APPLICATION
WINDOWS AND ICONS ON THE DESKTOP

- Choose the **Cascade** button to place the windows in an overlapping arrangement.
- Or choose the **Tile** button to place the windows side-by-side.
- Or choose the **Arrange Icons** to arrange the icons along the lower edge of the desktop.

See Also Applications, Control Menu, Dialog Boxes, Icons, Windows

TERMINAL

Terminal lets you connect your computer to other computers and exchange information via a modem.

TO START TERMINAL

Double-click the Terminal icon in the Accessories group of Program Manager.

TO SPECIFY THE COMMUNICATIONS SETTINGS

In order for two computers to communicate, both computers must be using the same communications settings (baud rate, data bits, stop bits, and parity). Furthermore, you must tell Terminal which port your modem is connected to. To set communications settings on your computer, choose **Settings ➤ Communications**. In the Communications dialog box, set the options needed by your system and the remote computer, then choose OK.

EXAMPLE The Communications dialog box below is set up for 2400 N-8-1 (2400 baud, No parity, 8 data bits, 1 stop bit), common settings for many bulletin boards and PC-to-PC communications. The modem is assumed to be attached to com port 1.

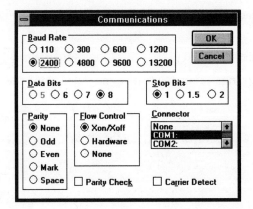

TO SPECIFY A PHONE NUMBER TO DIAL

1. Choose **Settings ➤** Phone **Number**.
2. Type the phone number you want in the Dial box.

3. Set any additional options you want, including timeout if not connected in a certain number of seconds, redial after timing out, and signal (beep) when connected.

4. Choose OK.

NOTE You can use parentheses and dashes to separate parts of the phone number. Type commas to insert delays. For example, the following string first dials 9, then pauses for 6 seconds, then dials the phone number:

9,,,1-800-555-1234

TO SELECT A MODEM AND CHANGE MODEM COMMAND SETTINGS

- Choose **Settings ➤ Modem Commands**. In the Modem Commands dialog box, choose the modem you're using and, if necessary, make any adjustments needed to the commands for your modem. Then choose OK.

NOTE Default modems include Hayes, MultiTech, TrailBlazer, and None. If you choose None, you'll need to define the Dial, Hangup, Binary Transmit (TX), Binary Receive (RX), and Originate commands for your modem. See your modem documentation for details on modem commands.

TO CHANGE THE PRINT SIZE AND SET OTHER PREFERENCES

1. Choose **Settings ➤ Terminal Preferences**. You'll see the Terminal Preferences dialog box shown below.

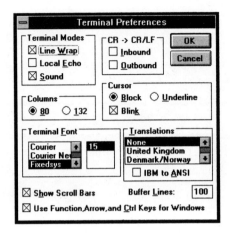

2. Under Terminal Font, choose a font and a size.

3. For most bulletin boards and information services, you can leave other options unchanged. If you're communicating with another PC, however, you might want to select the Terminal Echo, Inbound, and Outbound options.

TO PREPARE FOR A BINARY OR TEXT FILE TRANSFER

If you plan on transferring files, both computers should use the same communications protocols. To choose a communication protocol:

1. Choose **Settings ➤ Binary Transfers** for a binary transfer, or **Settings ➤ Text Transfers** for a text transfer.

2. Choose the options you want. The binary options are Xmodem/CRC or Kermit.

3. Choose OK. Now, follow the steps given below for sending or receiving files.

TO SAVE CURRENT COMMUNICATIONS SETTINGS, PHONE NUMBER, AND PREFERENCES

1. Choose **File ➤ Save**.

2. Enter a valid file name (no extension) that will make it easy to identify who the phone number and communications settings are for.

3. Choose OK.

Terminal automatically adds the extension .trm to the file name you provide.

TO CONNECT TO THE REMOTE COMPUTER

1. Turn on your modem (if necessary), and make sure all wires are properly connected.

2. Choose **File ➤ Open** and then double-click the name of the communications settings file you want to use.

3. Choose **Phone ➤ Dial**.

4. If you hear the remote computer answer, but get no response on your screen, try pressing ↵ once or twice.

5. Respond to whatever prompts the remote computer sends, by typing each reply and pressing ↵. Or, if you're connecting directly to another PC-compatible computer, you can "chat" with the person on the other end by typing text.

MAKING TERMINAL ANSWER THE PHONE

If another computer is calling your computer, and you're using a Hayes or Hayes-compatible modem with the ability to answer the phone, you can probably answer an incoming call by typing **ata** and pressing ↵ when you see RING on Terminal's screen. See Lesson 10, and the documentation for your modem for additional modem commands.

NOTE Text files are created with a text editor such as Notepad, and saved without any formatting characters except carriage returns and linefeeds. Binary files can contain any kind of data, including executable programs, formatted documents, or text. Unless speed is of utmost importance, you should *always* use binary transfer because it offers better error checking. Also keep in mind that programs such as PKZIP can compress your files so that they can be sent more quickly across telephone lines.

TO SEND A BINARY OR TEXT FILE

1. First, make sure you're connected with the remote computer. (If you're communicating with another PC, you should be able to type message back and forth.)

2. Choose **Transfers ➤ Send Binary File**, or **Transfers ➤ Send Text File**.

3. Select the file you want to send.

4. If you're sending a *text file*, and

   - To attach a linefeed to the end of each text line, select the Append LF check box.

   - To strip out linefeeds at the end of each line, select the Strip LF check box (the default).

5. Choose OK to begin sending the file.

TO RECEIVE A BINARY OR TEXT FILE

1. If you're communicating with a bulletin board or information service, initiate that computer's download operation. If you're receiving a file from another PC, the other user should start sending the file.

2. Choose **Transfers ➤ Receive Binary File** or **Transfers ➤ Receive Text File**.

3. Specify the name of the file you want to receive. If you specify the name of an existing file, that file will be replaced.

4. If you're receiving a *text file*, you have these options:

   - To add incoming information to the end of the specified file, select the Append File check box.

   - To save all of the formatting codes, select the Save Controls check box.

   - To receive the incoming text in tabular format (where tab characters are inserted between incoming text that is separated by two or more consecutive spaces), select the Table Format check box.

5. Choose OK to begin receiving the file.

TO STOP, SUSPEND, OR RESUME THE FILE TRANSFER

- Choose the Stop button or choose **Transfers ➤ Stop** to stop the transfer.
- Or choose the Pause button or choose **Transfers ➤ Pause** to temporarily suspend the transfer (available for text transfers only).
- Or choose the Resume button or choose **Transfers ➤ Resume** to resume a suspended transfer (available for text transfers only).

TO VIEW A TEXT FILE
BEFORE OR AFTER TRANSFERRING IT

1. Choose **Transfers ➤ View Text File**.
2. Select the file you want to view. Then do one of the following:
   - To attach a linefeed to the end of each text line, select the Append LF check box.
   - To strip out linefeeds at the end of each line, select the Strip LF check box.
3. Choose OK to copy the specified file onto the Terminal window.

NOTE As text is copied to the Terminal window, you can choose the usual Stop, Pause, or Resume buttons to control the output.

TO WORK WITH TEXT ON THE TERMINAL WINDOW

Optionally select the text you want to work with, then choose any of these options from the Edit menu.

- **Copy:** Copies selected text to the Clipboard.
- **Paste:** Pastes text from the Clipboard to the remote system.
- **Send:** Sends selected text to the remote system.

- **Select All**: Selects all text on the Terminal window and buffer.
- **Clear Buffer**: Clears all text from the Terminal window and buffer and frees memory.

NOTE When you type or receive more text than can fit in the window, Terminal places that text into a buffer. You can use the scroll bars to see text that isn't currently in view.

TO PRINT TEXT RECEIVED FROM THE REMOTE SYSTEM

- Choose **Settings ➤ Printer Echo** to print incoming text directly to the printer. Choose this option again if you need to eject a partial page from the printer.
- Or, select the text you want to print, copy it to the Clipboard, switch to a word processing or text-editor application, paste the contents of the Clipboard into a text file, then use the application's Print command.

TO DISCONNECT FROM THE REMOTE COMPUTER

1. If you're communicating with a bulletin board or information service, type whatever exit command the remote computer expects (e.g., **bye**). This severs the remote connection and ensures that your account isn't charged for additional connect time.
2. Choose **Phone ➤ Hangup** to hang up your modem.

TO SPECIFY THE TYPE OF TERMINAL TO EMULATE

- Choose **Settings ➤ Terminal Emulation**. Then select either TTY (Generic), DEC VT-100 (ANSI), or DEC VT-52. Choose OK.

See Also Lesson 10

VIRTUAL MEMORY

Windows uses *virtual memory* (disk space that acts as RAM) to temporarily transfer information currently in memory when it needs to free up memory for other information. To optimize performance, you can adjust the size, location, and type of the virtual memory (or *swap file*); or you can prevent Windows from using virtual memory altogether (recommended only if you're extremely short of disk space, since this slows down performance).

TO CHANGE THE DRIVE, TYPE, AND SIZE OF YOUR SWAP FILE

1. Double-click Control Panel in the Main group of Program Manager, then double-click the 386 Enhanced icon.

2. Choose the Virtual Memory button. The Virtual Memory dialog appears, showing the current settings.

3. Choose the Change>> button to expand the Virtual Memory dialog box.

4. Change the settings as required.

5. Choose OK. You'll see a dialog box telling you to restart Windows.

6. Choose the Restart button.

EXAMPLE Here's the expanded Virtual Memory dialog box after we chose the Change>> button.

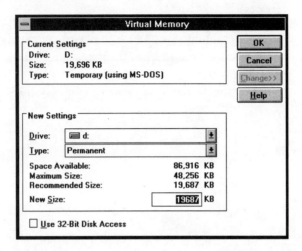

NOTE Choose the Help button in the Virtual Memory dialog box, or refer to your Windows documentation for details on changing swap file settings.

NOTE For more information, use Write to open the SYSINI.WRI file.

See Also 386 Enhanced Mode, Control Panel, Notepad, Write

WINDOWS

A window is any framed area on the screen. A closed window is called an *icon*. You can have many opened windows and icons on the desktop at once.

TO SELECT OR "ACTIVATE" A WINDOW OR ICON

- ◆ Click on the window or icon you want.

- ◆ Or, to cycle through application windows and icons, hold down the Alt key and repeatedly press Tab until you reach the window or icon name you want, then release the Alt key.

- ◆ Or, to switch to an application, open the Task List (press Ctrl+Esc) and choose an application from the list.

- ◆ Or, to cycle through document windows and icons, repeatedly press Ctrl+F6.

NOTE Before performing any other operation with a window or icon, you must first select it. The borders and menu bar will darken when a window is selected. The icon's label will darken when an icon is selected.

TO ARRANGE MULTIPLE OPEN APPLICATION WINDOWS AND ICONS

- ◆ Call up Task List by pressing Ctrl+Esc or double-clicking the desktop. Then choose **Window ➤ Tile** or **Window ➤ Cascade.** (See Lessons 1 and 2.)

NOTE The Tile and Cascade options let you see at least part of every open window and are handy for uncovering open windows that seem to have "disappeared." Many applications, including Program Manager, include a Window menu with Tile and Cascade options, which affect only document windows within the current application window.

See Also Windows at a Glance inside the front cover of this book.

W

WINDOWS SETUP

When first installing Windows, you used Windows Setup to install Windows and provide information about your hardware and software. After installing Windows, you can run Setup from Windows to:

- Change hardware options, including the display, keyboard, mouse, and network in use.

- Install device drivers not supplied with Windows.

- Set up applications that are already on your hard disk for use with Windows (described below).

- Add or remove optional Windows components (described below).

To install an updated version of a device driver that you previously installed, or change the Codepage setting for Windows, you must quit Windows and run Setup from the MS-DOS prompt. See your Windows documentation for more information.

Note that many Windows applications have setup programs of their own, and you should refer to the documentation that comes with each Windows application to find out how to install it. An application's setup program should not be run at the same time you're running Windows Setup.

TO START WINDOWS SETUP

1. If you're installing new hardware, quit all applications (except Program Manager).

2. Double-click the Windows Setup icon in the Main group of Program Manager.

EXAMPLE Here's the Windows Setup dialog box.

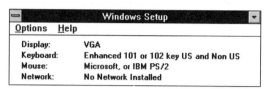

TO SET UP AN APPLICATION
AFTER WINDOWS IS INSTALLED

1. From the Windows Setup menu, choose **Options ➤ Set Up Applications**. You'll see the Setup Applications dialog box.

2. To search the hard disk for applications, select **Search For Applications**. Or, to specify a particular application, select **Ask You To Specify An Application**.

3. If you selected **Search For Applications**, select the drive or path you want to search from the next dialog box that appears, then choose the Search Now button. Skip to Step 5.

4. If you selected **Ask You To Specify An Application**, another dialog box appears. Type the path and filename of the application into the Application Path and Filename text box (or use the Browse button to locate the file). To install the selected application in a different program group, select that group from the Add to Program Group drop-down list box (the default group is Applications). Choose OK.

5. When setting up a non-Windows application, Setup looks for a PIF based on the application's base filename.

   ◆ If more than one PIF exists for a given filename, Setup displays a dialog box asking you to specify the one you want. Select the description you want and choose OK.

   ◆ If Setup doesn't find a PIF, it searches for information it needs to create one. If it finds the information, it asks whether you want Windows to use that information to create a PIF. Choose Yes.

   ◆ If Setup doesn't find a PIF and can't create one, Windows uses the default PIF, named _DEFAULT.PIF, when you start the application.

6. If you selected **Ask You To Specify An Application** in Step 2, skip to Step 9. If you selected **Search For Applications**, you'll see a dialog box showing all the applications that Setup recognizes.

7. Select one or more applications from the list on the left, then choose the Add button to copy the selected name(s) to the list on the right. Or, to copy all the applications, choose the Add All button. If you change your mind about setting up an application, select the application from the list on the right and choose the Remove button to return it to the list on the left.

8. Choose OK.

9. Windows Setup adds a program-item icon to the Applications group (or whatever group you specified in Step 4) for each selected application. If the Applications group doesn't exist, Setup creates it. Setup also creates a corresponding PIF for non-Windows applications.

NOTE After setting up the applications, you can move the icons to different groups if you wish.

TO ADD OR REMOVE
OPTIONAL WINDOWS COMPONENTS

1. From the Windows Setup menu, choose **Options ➤ Add/Remove Windows Components**. You'll see a dialog box like the one below listing the optional components. The name of each component that's currently on your disk is marked with an "X." These components can be removed. Components not marked with an "X" are not currently on your disk and can be added.

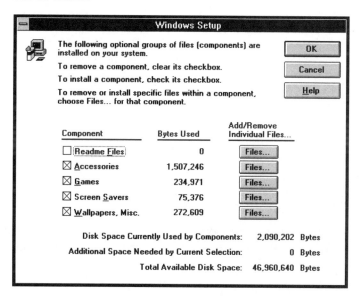

2. Decide which components you want to add or delete:

   ◆ To add an entire component (e.g., all Readme files), select the check box next to it. Or, to delete an entire component, clear the check box. Continue with Step 5.

   ◆ Or, to add or delete just part of a component, choose the Files button next to the component. You'll see a dialog box like this one. Continue with Step 3.

289

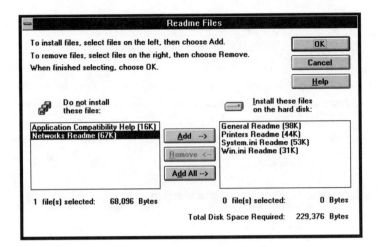

3. Select one or more files from the list on the left, then choose the Add button to copy the selected name(s) to the list on the right. Or, to add or delete all the files, choose the Add All button. If you change your mind about adding a file, select the file from the list on the right and choose the Remove button to return it to the list on the left.

4. Choose OK to return to the Windows Setup dialog box.

5. Choose OK to add or remove the selected files.

6. If you are adding components, you'll be asked to insert the appropriate Windows version 3.1 disk into your floppy disk drive. If necessary, type in a different drive letter, insert the disk into the drive, then choose OK to continue.

7. If you are deleting files, you'll be asked to confirm the deletions. Choose the Yes button to delete each file individually, or Yes To All to delete all the files at once, or No to skip the file without deleting.

See Also Lesson 2, Appendix, Icons, PIF Editor

WRITE

Write is a mini word-processor for creating and printing small documents for business and personal use.

TO START WRITE

- ◆ Double-click on the Write icon in the Accessories group of Program Manager.

EXAMPLE The example below combines fonts, styles, and a picture.

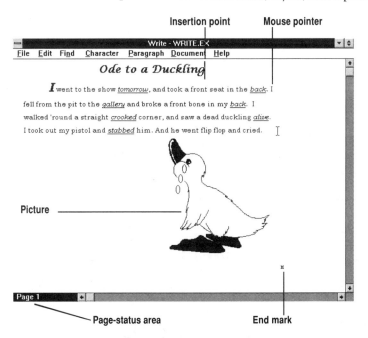

Insertion point   Mouse pointer

Picture

Page-status area   End mark

NOTE In the Write window, the *insertion point* indicates where text will appear when you start typing. The *end mark* indicates the end of a document (there is no text to the right of or below the end mark). The *page-status area* indicates the current page number after you have broken your document into pages. The *mouse pointer* indicates where the mouse is pointing inside the window and where the insertion point will move if you click in the document.

291

TO TYPE TEXT INTO YOUR DOCUMENT

♦ Just position the insertion point, then start typing.

TO SELECT TEXT

Use any of the techniques described in Lesson 5 or under Keyboard Shortcuts and Selecting Text in this Reference. You can also use the *selection area* in the left margin as follows:

♦ To select a line, click once in the left margin next to the line.

♦ To select several lines, move the mouse pointer into the left margin next to the first line to select. Then drag the mouse pointer through all the lines.

♦ To select a paragraph, move the insertion point into the left margin next to the paragraph, then double-click.

♦ To select several paragraphs, double-click in the left margin next to the first paragraph you want to select, then drag the mouse pointer through additional paragraphs, or hold down the Shift key and double-click next to each additional paragraph that you want to select.

♦ To select a range of text, click in the left margin next to the line where you want to begin the selection. Then move the insertion point to the end of the selection. Hold down the Shift key and click.

♦ To select the entire document, move the mouse pointer into the left margin, hold down the Ctrl key, then click.

♦ To deselect text, click anywhere in the document.

TO SEARCH FOR OR REPLACE TEXT

1. Position the insertion point where you want the search to start.

2. Choose **Find ➤ Find** if you're searching for text (the Find dialog box appears). Or choose **Find ➤ Replace** if you want to replace text (the Replace dialog box appears).

3. In the Find What box, type the text you want to search for.

4. If you chose **Find ➤ Replace**, type the replacement text into the Replace With box.

5. To match only whole words during the search, select the Match Whole Word Only check box.

6. To match capitalization exactly, select the Match Case check box.

7. Choose one of the following buttons (only Find Next is available for a Find):

  ◆ **Find Next**: Selects the next occurrence of the text you entered in Step 3. To edit the text, point to it on the document window and click the mouse.

  ◆ **Replace**: Replaces the selected text with the text you entered in Step 4 and waits for you to choose another button.

  ◆ **Replace All** or **Replace Selection**: Replace All automatically changes all occurrences of the text you entered in Step 3 to the text you entered in Step 4. Replace Selection replaces just the currently selected text.

8. Repeat Step 7 as needed.

9. When you're finished, choose the Cancel button from the Find dialog box, or the Close button from the Replace dialog box.

NOTE The search begins at the insertion point, or at the end of any selected text. When Write reaches the end of the document, it continues searching from the beginning of the document to where the search first started. You can use any of the following special characters in the Find What box (where ^ means the caret symbol—Shift+6).

TYPE	TO REPRESENT
?	Any character at this position. For example, *hea?* matches *health, head, theatrical,* and so forth. The question mark is a wildcard that means "at least one character."
^w	A space at this position.
^t	A Tab character at this position.

TYPE	TO REPRESENT
^p	A paragraph mark (⏎) at this position.
^d	A manual page break (Ctrl+⏎) at this position.
^	A caret at this position.

To repeat the last Find after closing the Find or Replace dialog box, choose **Find ➤ Repeat Last Find** or press F3.

TO INSERT OPTIONAL HYPHENS

- Press Ctrl+Shift+- (hyphen) at each desired hyphenation point. Optional hyphens are invisible unless they appear at the end of a line.

TO MOVE OR SIZE A PICTURE OR OTHER OBJECT

1. Click the object to select it.

2. To move the object, choose **Edit ➤ Move**. To enlarge or shrink an object, choose **Edit ➤ Size**. A square cursor appears at the center of the picture, and a dotted frame surrounds the picture.

3. Without pressing the mouse button, do one of the following:

   - To move the object, move the mouse right or left until the frame is where you want the object to appear.

   - To size the object, move the cursor to the corner of the outline, then move the mouse until the outline is the size you want. Moving the mouse left or right changes the width of the object; moving it up or down changes the length; and moving it diagonally changes both the length and the width.

   - To cancel the move or size, press Esc.

4. When the frame is the way you want it, click the mouse button or press ⏎.

EXAMPLE In this example, we're reducing the size of the picture.

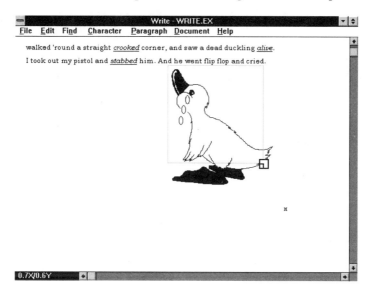

NOTE As an alternative to moving a picture, you can use the Left, Centered, or Right options on the Paragraph menu. When you size an object, the lower-left corner of the Write window displays sizing information in the form of *x* and *y* location values. To prevent distortion of the picture, keep these values as whole numbers (e.g., 3 instead of 0.3).

TO BREAK A DOCUMENT INTO PAGES

- ◆ Choose **File ➤ Repaginate**. To confirm each page break as repagination takes place, select the Confirm Page Breaks check box. Then choose OK.

- ◆ Or position the insertion point where you want a *manual* page break, then press Ctrl+↵. You can select, delete, or copy a manual page break like any other character in a document.

- ◆ Or print the document.

NOTE Printing automatically repaginates the document without asking you to confirm page breaks. If you chose **File ➤ Repaginate and Confirm Page Breaks**, Write pauses at each page break that it proposes to insert and at page breaks you inserted manually. You can then choose the following buttons:

- **Up**: Moves the page break up a line each time you choose the button.
- **Down**: Moves the page break down a line each time you choose the button. You can only move a page break down if you previously moved it up.
- **Confirm**: Accept this page break and move on to the next one.
- **Cancel**: Cancel the remaining repagination.

Each time Write pauses at a manual page break, it displays another dialog box that lets you keep or remove the page break.

Automatic page breaks inserted when you print or repaginate appear in the selection area of the Write window as arrows (>>).

Manual page breaks that you insert by pressing Ctrl+↵ or by moving the page breaks during repagination appear as a dotted line across the screen (the dotted line isn't printed).

After breaking the document into pages, you can move the insertion point to a specific page: Choose **Find ➤ Go To Page**, then type the page number you want and choose OK.

TO FORMAT CHARACTERS IN YOUR DOCUMENT

1. Position the insertion point where you want the new formatting to begin, or select the text that you want to format.

2. Open the Character menu. Then,

   - To select a style, choose **Bold, Italic, Underline, Superscript,** or **Subscript** from the menu. A check mark appears next to the selected style on the menu. Choosing the style again cancels the style and removes the check mark. You can select several styles at once by repeatedly choosing style options from the Character menu.

◆ To remove all character styles at once, choose Regular or press F5.

◆ To change the font to the next smaller or larger size (as determined by Write), choose **Reduce Font** or **Enlarge Font**.

◆ To change the font or point size, choose **Fonts**. Then, from the Fonts dialog box that appears, select the name of the font you want, the font style (regular, bold, bold italic, or italic), and the point size. Then choose OK.

EXAMPLE Here's a sample Fonts dialog box with a font name, style, and point size selected.

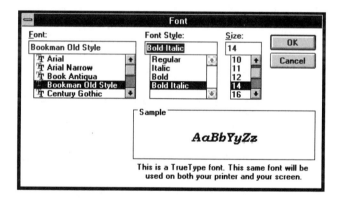

TO FORMAT PARAGRAPHS

1. Place the insertion point inside the paragraph you want to change, or select a group of paragraphs if you want to change the format of several at once.

2. To use the Ruler to format the paragraph, choose **Document ➤ Ruler On** to display the ruler. (Choosing **Document ➤ Ruler Off** hides the Ruler again.)

3. Change the formatting as described below, either by using the Ruler or by choosing the equivalent options from the Paragraph or Document menu.

EXAMPLE The Ruler lets you change the alignment, spacing, indentation, and tabs for a paragraph.

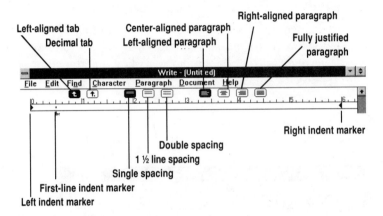

NOTE A new paragraph starts out with the same format as the previous paragraph. To remove a paragraph mark, place the insertion point at the beginning of the paragraph that follows the mark you want to delete, then press Backspace.

When you copy or move a paragraph, you should include the paragraph mark in the selection to keep the paragraph formats with the paragraph.

TO CHANGE PARAGRAPH ALIGNMENT OR LINE SPACING

- ◆ In the Ruler, click on the icon that represents the alignment or line spacing you want.
- ◆ Or open the Paragraph menu. Then choose the **Left, Centered, Right,** or **Justified** alignment option; or choose the **Single Space, 1 1/2 Space,** or **Double Space** line spacing option.

TO CHANGE PARAGRAPH INDENTS

- In the Ruler, drag the left indent, first-line indent, or right indent marker to a new position.

- Or choose **Paragraph ➤ Indents**. Then type a measurement for any indent you want to change. Choose OK when you're finished.

NOTE Initially, the left indent and first-line indent settings are the same, with the left indent marker appearing as a small dot (•) on top of the left indent marker (➤).

You can create a *hanging indent*, where the first line extends farther to the left than the rest of a paragraph, as in a numbered or bulleted list. To do so, drag the left indent marker on the Ruler so that it's *to the right of* the first-line indent marker. If you're using the Indents dialog box, type a positive number in the Left Indent box and a negative number in the First Line indent box.

After setting a hanging indent, you might also want to set a Tab at the same location as the left indent marker. This would allow you to type the number or bullet character for a list item, press Tab, and then type the remaining text for the list item.

In addition to indenting text, you can also indent objects that you've copied, linked, or embedded in your document.

TO SET TABS

- In the Ruler, click the icon for the type of tab you want (either left-aligned or decimal). Then click the Ruler where you want to set the tab; or drag an existing tab marker to a new position on the Ruler. To delete a tab, drag the tab marker down off the Ruler then release the mouse button.

- Or, choose **Document ➤ Tabs**. In the Tabs dialog box, click a Positions box. Then type, change, or delete a measurement for the tab stop, relative to the left margin. To set a decimal tab, select the Decimal check box below the measurement you enter. Then choose OK.

EXAMPLE Here's a Ruler and its equivalent Tabs dialog box. The settings are the same in both.

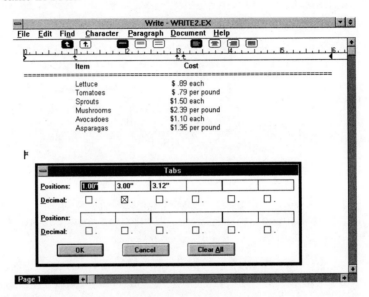

NOTE Unlike paragraph alignment, indents, and line spacing (which can be set for individual paragraphs), tab settings apply to the *entire* document.

Tabs are preset at every half inch; however, preset tabs do not appear on the Ruler or in the Tabs dialog box. You can define up to 12 tabs, which will override the preset tabs.

To clear all tabs at once, choose the Clear All button in the Tabs dialog box.

To align text at the tab stop, position the insertion point in your document, press the Tab key, then type your text.

When you type text at a decimal tab stop, the characters appear to the left of the tab stop until you type a decimal point (.). The decimal point is inserted at the tab stop, with additional characters appearing to the right of the decimal point.

TO ADD HEADERS AND FOOTERS TO A DOCUMENT

1. Choose **Document ➤ Header** to add a header, or **Document ➤ Footer** to add a footer.

2. In the blank Header or Footer window, type the text you want, just as if you were editing in the document. You can format text as usual.

3. To set options in the Page Header or Page Footer dialog box, click the dialog box, then:

   - To adjust the distance between the header or footer and the edge of the page, type a measurement in the Distance From Top or Distance From Bottom box.

   - To place the header or footer on the first page of the printed document, select the Print On First Page check box. (Otherwise, the header or footer starts on the second page.)

   - To insert a page number at the insertion point position, choose the Insert Page # button.

   - To clear the header or footer window, choose the Clear button.

4. When you're finished editing the header or footer, choose the Return To Document button from the dialog box, or press Esc.

EXAMPLE After choosing **Document ➤ Header**, we right-aligned the header by choosing **Paragraph ➤ Right**, typing *Ode to a duckling*, pressing the Tab key, typing *Page* followed by a space, then choosing the Insert Page # button from the Page Header dialog box. We next pressed ↵ three times to add some blank lines, then pressed Esc to return to the document.

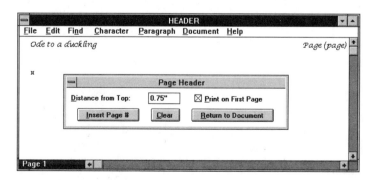

NOTE The page header or footer appears when you print the document. If the header, footer, or margins are too close to the end of the page, the printer may not be able to print them.

To edit an existing header or footer, simply choose the **Document ➤ Header** or **Document ➤ Footer** options again and make any necessary changes.

TO CHANGE THE PAGE LAYOUT SETTINGS FOR AN ENTIRE DOCUMENT

- ◆ Choose **Document ➤ Page Layout**, fill in the Page Layout dialog box, then choose OK.

EXAMPLE Here's the Page Layout dialog box with the default settings.

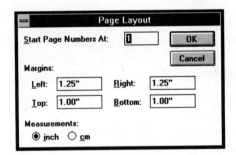

TO PRINT THE DOCUMENT IN THE WRITE WINDOW

- ◆ Choose **File ➤ Print**, select the options you want, then choose OK.

EXAMPLE Here's the Print dialog box.

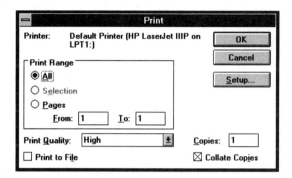

NOTE Options in the Print dialog box are:

◆ **Print Range**: All prints the entire document (default). Selection prints just the selected text in the document. Pages prints just the pages specified in the From and To boxes.

◆ **Print Quality**: Controls the quality of printed graphic images. Available options depend on your printer.

◆ **Print to File**: Saves output to a file. After you choose the OK button, you'll be prompted for the filename.

◆ **Copies**: Controls the number of copies printed.

◆ **Collate Copies**: Separates each document page when printing multiple copies (if your printer supports this feature).

To change printers and print options, you can choose the Setup button in the Print dialog box, or choose **File ➤ Print Setup**.

See Also Lesson 5, Clipboard; Cut and Paste; Keyboard Shortcuts; Notepad; Object Linking and Embedding; Object Packager; Selecting Text

APPENDIX

*I*NSTALLING WINDOWS

This Appendix takes you through the steps for performing a basic installation (called Express Setup; advanced users who want to fine-tune the system can run a Custom Setup) of Windows 3.1. Before you begin, make sure you have sufficient hardware to run Windows 3.1.

HARDWARE REQUIREMENTS FOR WINDOWS 3.1

To use Windows 3.1, you need *at least* the following:

- ◆ An IBM PC or compatible computer with an 80286 microprocessor for Standard mode, or a 386 or 486 processor for 386 Enhanced mode.

- ◆ 1MB RAM (640K conventional memory + 384K extended memory) for Standard mode. For 386 Enhanced mode, a bare minimum of 2MB RAM (640K conventional + 1024K extended memory) is required, though a minimum of 4MB RAM is more realistic.

- ◆ A hard disk with 8 to 10 MB of *available* storage space.

- ◆ An EGA, VGA, 8514/A or equivalent graphics adapter (VGA recommended).

- ◆ A mouse is optional, but highly recommended and required for certain applications (such as Paintbrush). This book assumes that you're using a mouse.

INSTALLING WINDOWS

To install Windows 3.1, gather up the floppy disks that make up the entire Windows 3.1 program. Then do the following:

1. Start your computer in the usual manner, and get to the DOS command prompt (typically **C:\>**).

2. Insert the Windows installation disk #1 in drive A (or B for 3.5-inch disks). For drive A, close the drive door.

3. Type **a:** (or **b:**) and press ↵ to switch drives (the prompt should change to **A:\>** or something similar).

4. Type **setup** and press ↵.

5. Read the installation information that appears, and press ↵ to proceed.

6. When given the options Custom Setup and Express Setup, choose Express Setup (unless you're an experienced user and want to customize your installation).

Setup checks your current configuration and suggests a drive and directory for installing (typically c:\windows). Just press ↵ to proceed. Setup then begins copying files, and informs you when you need to change floppy disks. Eventually, you'll be prompted to enter your name and company name. Type in your complete name. Optionally, press Tab, then type in your company name. Press ↵ when done. You'll be given a chance to confirm, and optionally change, your entry before the installation procedure continues.

INSTALLING PRINTERS

As you progress through the installation procedure, you'll be prompted to install a printer. Use the arrow keys or scroll bars to highlight the name of your printer. Then choose Install or press ↵.

Next, you'll be asked which port the printer is connected to. Choose the appropriate port (typically LPT1:) then choose Install or press ↵.

INSTALLING APPLICATIONS

Near the end of the installation procedure, Windows will start searching your hard disk for applications, and creating icons for those applications automatically. Follow the instructions on the screen until you get to the dialog box asking if you want to take the Windows tutorial. As noted in Lesson 1, this tutorial gives valuable practice in working with the Windows interface. If you don't run it now, you can do so at any time by choosing **Help ➤ Windows Tutorial** from the Program Manager menu.

COMPLETING THE INSTALLATION

When the installation procedure is complete, you'll see a message telling you so. Remove the floppy that's currently in drive A or B, then click the Reboot button (or press ↵).

IS IT INSTALLED?

To verify that you've installed Windows 3.1, type **win** and press ↵ at the DOS command prompt after rebooting. If you see a sign-on screen for Windows 3.0 rather than version 3.1, don't panic. It may simply be that Windows 3.1 is still using your old Windows 3.0 graphics driver.

When you get to the Windows Program Manager, you can check to see which version of Windows you're really using. Choose Help from Program Manager's menu bar (by pressing Alt+H or clicking that option). Then choose About Program Manager (by typing A or clicking that option). If you're indeed using Windows 3.1, the resulting dialog box will look something like Figure A.1. Choose OK or press ↵ to leave the dialog box.

If you are still using a Windows 3.0 graphics driver, you may find that lines of text disappear from time to time. Contact your display manufacturer for information on getting an updated Windows 3.1 graphics driver for your monitor.

Now you can proceed to Lesson 1 and start learning your way around the Windows 3.1 desktop.

FIGURE A.1:

The About Program Manager dialog box for Windows 3.1.

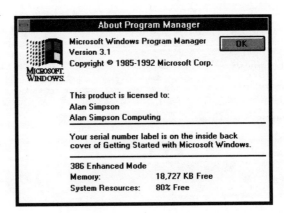

INDEX

Note: In this index, page numbers in **boldface** type show where you'll find the primary discussion of an important Windows topic; page numbers in regular type point to further information. Page numbers in *italic* type point to illustrations.

Numbers and Symbols

386 Enhanced mode, **158**
    defining shortcut keys in, **136–137**
    DOS applications and, 35, 186
>> (angle brackets)
    in dialog boxes, 185
    in Write, 296
\ (backslash)
    in path names, 190
    root directory and, 189
^ (caret search character), 294
: (colon)
    bypassing sign-on logo with, 138
    in drive names, 188
^d (manual page break search character), 294
... (ellipses), after menu commands, 219
- (hyphen)
    opening Control menu with, 178
    in Write, 294
^p (paragraph mark search character), 294
. (period), in filenames, 189
+ (plus sign), in icons, 188
? (question mark), as search character, 293
/ (forward slash), selecting all files with, 194
^t (Tab search character), 293
^w (space search character), 293

A

About Program Manager dialog box, *308*
Accessories window, *135*
activating windows, 26–27, 285
Add Fonts dialog box, *201*, 201
adding
    cards to Cardfile, 53–54, 169, 172
    colors to graphics, 89
    fonts, 201
    graphics to Cardfile cards, 171
    instructions to packages, 113
    printers, 259
    time and date to documents, 226
    Windows components, 289–290
Alarm Controls dialog box, 61
alignment, in Write, 298
Alt key
    activating windows, 26, 29
    exiting applications, 33, 34
    exiting Help, 210
    linking, 233
    moving files, 125
    navigating in dialog boxes, 182
    opening Control menu, 178–179
    opening list boxes, 184
    opening menus, 9, 218

B

backslash (\ )
    in path names, 190
    root directory and, 189
Backspace key, 72
base names, file, 189
batch files, 225, 226
binary file transfers, *144*, 144, 147, 278, 280
bitmap graphics, 84. *See also* graphics
    saving captured screens as, 256–257
Bitstream, MakeUp program, 81–82, 114
.BMP files, 256–257
boldface type style, 296–297
Bookmark Define dialog box, *207*
bookmarks, Help system, 207–208
Box tool, Paintbrush, *238*, 243
branches, directory, 117, 118
Break key, 265
Brush tool, Paintbrush, *238*, 242
bypassing
    DOS, 139
    File Manager, 133
    sign-on logo, 138
    startup applications, 138

C

Calculator, **63–65**, *64*, **162–163**, *162*, *163*
Calendar, 46, **57–63**, *58*, **164–169**, *164*, *165*
    annotating dates, 166
    autoloading appointments, 133
    choosing views, 58–60
    Day settings, 167
    Day view, 59, *164*, 164–165
    deleting appointments, 168
    entering appointments, 60–62, 166

marking dates, 168
    Month view, *59*, 60, *165*, 165
    opening saved appointments, 62
    printing appointments, 62, 62–63, 168
    saving appointments, 62, 169
    setting alarm, 60–61, *61*, 63, 166–167
    special time settings, 167
    starting, 164–165
    viewing specific dates, 165–166
Cancel button, 10
captured screens. *See* screen images
Cardfile, **52–57**, *52*, *54*, **169–173**
    adding cards, 53–54, 169, 172
    adding graphics to cards, 171
    autoloading index cards, 55, **132–133**
    copying cards, 172
    deleting cards, 56, 172
    dialing telephone numbers, 169, 172–172
    editing cards, 172
    exiting, *57*, 57
    graphics in, 56, 65–66, 171
    List view versus Card view, 170
    modems and, 53, 169
    moving through cards, 170
    OLE and, 101, 228–231
    opening card files, 55, 57
    organizing information with, 65, 66
    printing cards, 172
    saving cards, 54–55
    searching in, 56, 171
    starting, 169
    using cards, 55–56
caret search character (^), 294
cascading icons, 275, 285
cascading windows, 30–32, *32*, 285
CD-ROM drives, 117, 154
Character Map accessory, **77–80**, *78*, **173–175**
character styles, 296–297
characters, special, 77–80, 173–175

M

W

X

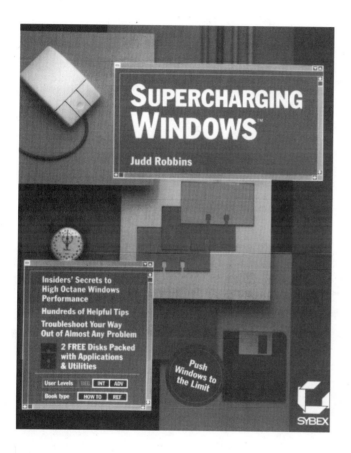

Help Yourself with Another Quality Sybex Book

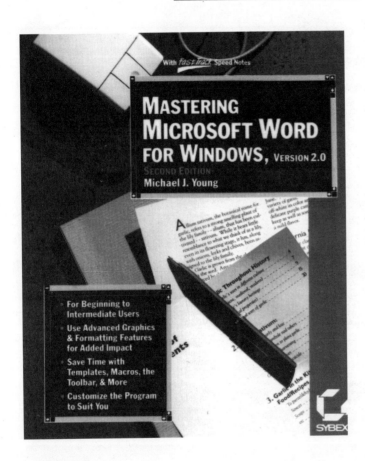

Mastering Microsoft Word for Windows,

Version 2.0

Second Edition

Michael J. Young

Here is an up-to-date new edition of our complete guide to Word for Windows, featuring the latest software release. It offers a tutorial for newcomers, and hands-on coverage of intermediate to advanced topics with desktop publishing skills emphasized. Special topics include: tables and columns, fonts, graphics, Styles and Templates, macros, and multiple windows.

596pp; 7 1/2" x 9"
ISBN: 0-7821-1012-6

Available
at Better
Bookstores
Everywhere

Sybex. Help Yourself.

SYBEX

FREE BROCHURE!

Complete this form today, and we'll send you a full-color brochure of Sybex bestsellers.

Please supply the name of the Sybex book purchased.

_____

How would you rate it?

_____ Excellent   _____ Very Good   _____ Average   _____ Poor

Why did you select this particular book?

_____ Recommended to me by a friend
_____ Recommended to me by store personnel
_____ Saw an advertisement in _____
_____ Author's reputation
_____ Saw in Sybex catalog
_____ Required textbook
_____ Sybex reputation
_____ Read book review in _____
_____ In-store display
_____ Other _____

Where did you buy it?

_____ Bookstore
_____ Computer Store or Software Store
_____ Catalog (name: _____
_____ Direct from Sybex
_____ Other: _____

Did you buy this book with your personal funds?

_____ Yes   _____ No

About how many computer books do you buy each year?

_____ 1-3   _____ 3-5   _____ 5-7   _____ 7-9   _____ 10+

About how many Sybex books do you own?

_____ 1-3   _____ 3-5   _____ 5-7   _____ 7-9   _____ 10+

Please indicate your level of experience with the software covered in this book:

_____ Beginner   _____ Intermediate   _____ Advanced

Which types of software packages do you use regularly?

_____ Accounting	_____ Databases	_____ Networks
_____ Amiga	_____ Desktop Publishing	_____ Operating Systems
_____ Apple/Mac	_____ File Utilities	_____ Spreadsheets
_____ CAD	_____ Money Management	_____ Word Processing
_____ Communications	_____ Languages	_____ Other _____

(please specify)

Which of the following best describes your job title?

_____ Administrative/Secretarial _____ President/CEO

_____ Director _____ Manager/Supervisor

_____ Engineer/Technician _____ Other _____
(please specify)

Comments on the weaknesses/strengths of this book: _____

_____

_____

_____

_____

Name _____

Street _____

City/State/Zip _____

Phone _____

PLEASE FOLD, SEAL, AND MAIL TO SYBEX

-- -- -- -- -- -- -- -- -- -- -- -- -- -- -- -- -- -- -- --

SYBEX, INC.
Department M
2021 CHALLENGER DR.
ALAMEDA, CALIFORNIA USA
94501

SYBEX

SEAL

THE CHARACTER MAP

The Character Map is discussed in Lesson 5. As an alternative method of typing special characters, you can do the following:

1. In your document, choose the character's font; i.e., Symbol or Wingdings for column 3 or 4, or any TrueType font for column 2.

2. For characters 33 through 126, type the text character from column 2. For example, typing ! when Wingdings is the current font produces the pencil character.

   For characters 128 and higher, turn on Num Lock, hold down the Alt key, type the four-digit character number, and release the Alt key. For example, selecting Wingdings and then using Alt and the numeric keypad to type 0255 produces the flying-window character.

Alt+KEY number	TrueType text font	TrueType Symbol font	TrueType WingDings font	Alt+KEY number	TrueType text font	TrueType Symbol font	TrueType WingDings font	Alt+KEY number	TrueType text font	TrueType Symbol font	TrueType WingDings font
33	!	!		55	7	7		77	M	M	
34	"	∀		56	8	8		78	N	N	
35	#	#		57	9	9		79	O	O	
36	$	∃		58	:	:		80	P	Π	
37	%	%		59	;	;		81	Q	Θ	
38	&	&		60	<	<		82	R	P	
39	'	∋		61	=	=		83	S	Σ	
40	(	(		62	>	>		84	T	T	
41	)	)		63	?	?		85	U	Y	
42	*	∗		64	@	≅		86	V	ς	
43	+	+		65	A	A		87	W	Ω	
44	,	,		66	B	B		88	X	Ξ	
45	-	−		67	C	X		89	Y	Ψ	
46	.	.		68	D	Δ		90	Z	Z	
47	/	/		69	E	E		91	[	[	
48	0	0		70	F	Φ		92	\	∴	
49	1	1		71	G	Γ		93	]	]	
50	2	2		72	H	H		94	^	⊥	
51	3	3		73	I	I		95	_	_	
52	4	4		74	J	ϑ		96	`		
53	5	5		75	K	K		97	a	α	
54	6	6		76	L	Λ		98	b	β	